PUBLIC SPEAKING MADE SIMPLE

How to Overcome Your Fear of Public Speaking and Present with Confidence

By Michael H. Fleischner

Public Speaking Made Simple

Copyright © 2013

All rights reserved. No part of this book may be used or reproduced by any means, graphic, electronic, or mechanical including photocopying without the express written permission of the author.

Because of the dynamic nature of the Internet, any web address or links contained in this book may no longer be valid.

ISBN-13:
978-0615775142 (Made Simple Media)

ISBN-10:
0615775144

Please see page 103 for a special gift. Your feedback is important to me and I'd like to give you my Top 5 Public Speaking Pitfalls Sheet at no cost.

Free resources at http://www.publicspeakingsimple.com/

Dedicated to my loved ones—Jamie, Samantha, and Alex, as well as my father and brother, who continue to support all of my endeavors

In memory of my mother

Free resources at http://www.publicspeakingsimple.com/

Contents

Introduction... 7

Chapter 1: You Can Do This

My story... 10

Believe you can... 14

What most people won't tell you about anxiety... 17

The TODAY Show... 19

Conquering your fear... 22

    Believe it's possible... 23

    Reframe your anxiety... 28

    Proper breathing... 30

    Do it anyway... 31

Chapter 2: Powerful Lessons from Effective Speakers

    The rule of four... 35

    Mirror, mirror... 37

Free resources at http://www.publicspeakingsimple.com/

Videotaping... 39

Starting small... 40

Repetition... 43

Chapter 3: Strategies for a Winning Presentation

Beyond basic preparation... 49

Know your material... 52

Know your audience... 55

Overcome your habits... 57

Lay the groundwork... 60

Start an outline... 61

Chapter 4: Creating Your Winning Presentation

The introduction... 64

The core presentation... 69

The linear approach... 70

The nonlinear approach... 76

Free resources at http://www.publicspeakingsimple.com/

Subject matter expertise... 79

Effective formats and delivery methods... 84

    One-on-one presentations... 85

    Small-group presentations... 86

    Large-group presentations... 89

Online and Web-Based formats... 93

Public Speaking Made Simple strategies... 95

    Rehearse in your mind... 95

    Begin with a goal... 97

    Preparation... 98

    Expect to transition... 98

    Breathe... 99

    Have a presentation checklist... 100

    Get started... 101

Conclusion... 102

Free resources at http://www.publicspeakingsimple.com/

Introduction

It's no secret that public speaking is one of the most feared activities on the planet. Next to skydiving and other extreme sports, nothing creates anxiety like standing up in front of a group of strangers with all eyes upon you. In fact, public speaking is so feared that scholars have attached a label to it—glossophobia.

Countless studies show that public speaking is in fact anxiety producing. Anyone who's ever had to present in front of others has had a twinge of nervousness, anxiety, or some level of discomfort. Believe it or not, this is a natural reaction to stepping out into the unknown. In fact, some studies have even gone so far as to say the fear of public speaking is hardwired into our being. But fear not: so is the joy of having a positive experience on stage or in front of others. As someone who's spent many years working on and overcoming my own fear of public speaking, I can definitively say that once you conquer the fear of public speaking, presenting becomes much more enjoyable.

The purpose of *Public Speaking Made Simple* is to dispel many of your beliefs about speaking in public and teach you how to communicate effectively to any sized audience. In fact, as you begin to apply the public speaking secrets I reveal in this guide, you'll discover that public speaking can come easily and effortlessly. Just as you once struggled with learning to ride a bike or drive a car, then later enjoyed the benefits of conquering your own fear, effective public speaking becomes second nature—something you enjoy.

My goal is to make you into a confident, productive public speaker —whatever that entails for you. Not everyone wants the same thing. Some individuals want a public speaking career or choose to give presentations to large audiences. Others simply want the necessary confidence required to present a business plan or share a story with a group of

Free resources at http://www.publicspeakingsimple.com/

friends. Regardless of your goal, the techniques provided in the following pages can support you in any speech or presentation you choose.

The techniques I'm sharing with you in this book are designed to improve confidence, communication skills, and effectiveness when speaking in public. I'm going to share my personal story with you and provide a step-by-step roadmap to help you overcome your fear and present with confidence. The one thing I can't help you with is subject matter expertise—that's up to you. However, even if you're unsure about your topic, I'll give you some helpful strategies for creating a presentation designed to win over any audience. Before covering some powerful public speaking techniques, I'd like to share with you my own story of anxiety, fear, and insecurity when speaking in front of others.

Free resources at http://www.publicspeakingsimple.com/

Chapter 1

You Can Do This

Free resources at http://www.publicspeakingsimple.com/

My story

It's not hard for me to recall where my fear of public speaking began. I can still remember the first time I experienced discomfort when speaking in front of others. It started as early as the third grade, when I experienced extreme anxiety when my teacher asked me to stand up and read out loud in front of the class. Although reading out loud was a common practice when I went to school, the first time I was old enough to recall the sensations associated with the task left an indelible mark. Reading out loud seems like a relatively easy thing to do, but it was torture. There was an instant rush as I rose to my feet, and it wasn't long before I discovered my body trembling, my mouth extremely dry, and my face flushed. As I focused on these sensations, I grew even more anxious and felt as if I were going to pass out. As a third grader, all I remember was how uncomfortable I felt, and I immediately associated my physical symptoms with the task of standing up alone in front of others. From then on, my fear of public speaking only got worse. As a child, I never fully understood what was happening to me or why I was feeling this anxiety, but later in life I realized overcoming my anxiety was essential if I wanted to be successful.

In college and the workplace, this fear of public speaking still haunted me. As I got older, the divide between those who were comfortable in their own skin, who seemingly spoke with ease, and individuals like myself became all the more evident. In college the students who got the best grades were the ones who stood in front of the class, confident and relaxed, giving answers and presenting their material. All I wanted to do was hide behind someone else. There were a number of occasions when I asked my professors if I could avoid a presentation, giving them some lame excuse as to why it wasn't an option for me. The fear of public speaking was simply debilitating.

At work it was more of the same. After I graduated from college and got my first job, contributing and being part of a work team

Free resources at http://www.publicspeakingsimple.com/

was essential. It was even easier to notice those individuals who seemed to speak seamlessly and flawlessly as part of the group. And it was these individuals who got the promotions, accolades, and other rewards associated with socially effective communication. I knew that unless I could address my fear of public speaking in some way, advancing my career was not going to happen anytime soon.

Even though public speaking wasn't my strong suit, I did consider myself pretty confident in other areas of life. So why was I failing at this one task? It wasn't long before I started to ask myself some very basic questions: What do these people have that I do not? How are they able to be so comfortable in front of a group when I'm a nervous wreck? What would I have to do to become a confident, effective speaker? By asking the right questions, I soon began to find answers. Many of them were unexpected but truly valuable.

At the same time that I began my search for answers, I was fortunate enough to attend an author presentation at a local Barnes & Noble bookstore. Many years ago, bookstores were a great source for listening to authors and learning virtually anything you were interested in. I didn't know it at the time, but the individual who was presenting would become a long-time friend and mentor. He spoke with ease and confidence and was someone that I definitely wanted to be like. Most importantly, he would later help me understand that effective speaking was within my grasp and how to achieve my goal of becoming an effective public speaker.

Now I realize that much of my anxiety and fear of public speaking was caused by factors I thought were outside of my control. In addition to the physical symptoms, anxiety-provoking thoughts like "Everyone is judging me," "What if I mess up?" "What if I pass out?" "What if I pee in my pants?" "I think I'm going to die!" streaming through my mind only made matters worse. It didn't take long to realize that the more I paid attention to my internal dialog, the more anxious I got, the more my body

Free resources at http://www.publicspeakingsimple.com/

trembled, and the more embarrassed I became. Learning to cope with this anxiety was difficult for me without an easy to follow resource and it took many years to understand the causes and cure for breaking the cycle. The good news is that I'm going to take the years of trial and error that I had to experience on my own and share my most significant discoveries with you. Not only is this going to save you time spent figuring things out on your own, but you'll also benefit from my experience in finding the methods that make a permanent improvement in your ability to interact with others.

After that initial presentation at the Barnes and Noble bookstore, I hung back and introduced myself to my soon-to-be mentor. Our friendship grew quickly, and it wasn't long before he shared a number of his presentation techniques with me. As a former business owner, Alan spent most of his adult life consulting and speaking in front of large audiences—persuading them to support his goals. How did he do it? He made public speaking seem so easy and appear nearly effortless. I knew that if anyone could help me improve, it was him. In fact, he was the key to helping me overcome my fears and become a powerful speaker.

Based on my experience, it's vitally important to have a public speaking role model or mentor help you on your journey to public speaking success. For some people, having a mentor who can literally take you by the hand and work with you on a regular basis is ideal. For others who like to work alone, finding a hands-on mentor may not be the right approach, but realizing the importance of learning from others is paramount. Your mentor may take the form of a live person, videos, or speaking events. No matter what type of mentor you're most comfortable with, you need a clear picture of the type of speaker you want to become. Whose speaking style do you prefer? What type of speaker do you want to be? Are you striving to be a motivational speaker or someone who's simply comfortable in ad hoc speaking situations? With a clear picture of the person you want to become, the easier it is to be successful. Operating

Free resources at http://www.publicspeakingsimple.com/

without a specific goal is like a ship without a rudder: you're sure to end up on the rocks.

Once you know where you're going, it's time to chart how to get there. For me this started by watching others and identifying characteristics of powerful public speakers. Beginning with the end in mind helped me focus my efforts and start making progress. I don't know how long my complete transformation took because my focus was on making progress with each and every presentation. What I do know is that the anxiety associated with speaking was virtually gone within a number of months after truly getting started. Imagine being terrified of public speaking your whole life only to overcome those fears in a few short months. This is my goal for you—to help you realize that can conquering the fear of public speaking can become your reality. Expect to change slowly at first but more rapidly as you continue your journey. At some point you'll look back and realize just how far you've come. Focus on making small changes steadily over time and the journey becomes almost effortless.

One of the most important aspects of your transformation is having the right mind-set. My mentor made the parallel to golf, a game that is largely mental. Public speaking is the same way. You must focus on your internal beliefs and dialog long before you set foot onto the "stage". If you begin thinking differently about yourself and the art of public speaking you can get much farther much faster than you've ever imagined. You see most people never become powerful speakers because in their own minds, they don't believe it's possible and never expect it to happen. This is a natural tendency but one that can be overcome.

Did you know that Arnold Schwarzenegger, the Austria-born bodybuilding champion, actor, and politician, as a child filled his walls with pictures of bodybuilders in perfect form and focused on these images every day as he developed his own physical strength and abilities? Whether he knew it or not, he was

Free resources at http://www.publicspeakingsimple.com/

focusing on his inside game long before what he wanted materialized in his physical world. By applying similar techniques, you can change your mind. When you do, you're removing obstacles, changing potential, and making improvements in your physical world. Don't worry: I'm not trying to sell you on some mystical solution to your public speaking challenges. Rather, once you understand that the same thinking that got you where you are is not going to help you get to where you want to be, you'll recognize the need for a new mental game. With a new mind-set comes new opportunity.

Believe you can

True success only becomes possible if you can see yourself speaking with confidence. At this point, developing such an image may seem difficult, but if you can see yourself in your mind's eye speaking with confidence and conviction, then you can and will be successful—guaranteed! I understand if you have doubts at this point. If you had made this suggestion to me six months before I started my journey, I would have dismissed it quickly. However, it wasn't long before discovering why and how this could be one of the essential keys to success. Let me explain how this simple idea came into being and made a permanent transformation possible.

In addition to finding a mentor, I was also on the hunt for any information that would help me gain confidence and improve my ability to speak in front of others. It wasn't long before I found a group of people with a similar goal in my local area. The group I discovered was called Toastmasters, a nonprofit, nonreligious organization that helps individuals develop their public speaking and leadership skills through practice and feedback in local clubs across the globe. The organization was founded in 1924 and is still thriving today.

Free resources at http://www.publicspeakingsimple.com/

Those of you who are familiar with Toastmasters may have already had some experience with your local chapter or decided that the organization isn't for you. When first learning about the organization, I said to myself, "I could never get up in front of a group of strangers and give a speech. Also I'm not going to join a group that focuses solely on my biggest fear!" Unfortunately, that way of thinking kept me from attending any Toastmasters meetings for almost a year after learning about the group. Eventually I overcame my fear of seeking help and mustered up the courage to attend a meeting. It wasn't long before I started participating in my local Toastmasters chapter and enjoying all of the benefits it offered. Said another way I realized that my current mind-set of avoiding situations that could potentially help me wasn't moving me toward my goal or conquering my fear.

I'm not here to tell you that Toastmasters is your key to success and in fact, some individuals never become comfortable with Toastmasters or perhaps have a less than desirable experience. Others don't follow the beginner's program to the letter. I'm a great example of the latter because even though I attended a number of Toastmasters meetings, technically I did not "graduate." To do so you must deliver a set number of speeches to the chapter. After presenting on a number of occasions, I felt so confident in my presentation abilities that graduating in the traditional sense was no longer important to me. My goal here is to simply make you aware that supportive environments exist, and if you're in a hurry to overcome your fear of public speaking, Toastmasters provides some very good resources to help. It's also a great place to find a mentor if you're struggling to find one in the area of public speaking.

At the time I was considering attending Toastmasters, my full=time job was running business development for a leading publisher. After a series of anxiety-producing presentations, I finally gave in and went to my first meeting. As afraid as I was to attend a Toastmasters gathering, continuing to experience extreme anxiety when giving presentations at work was no

Free resources at http://www.publicspeakingsimple.com/

longer an option for me. The thought of going to a meeting at this point seemed like a better option than having to stand up in front of my colleagues and experience the physical and emotional discomfort I felt while giving a presentation.

Socially I'm not a big fan of crowds or being in unfamiliar situations – but that didn't stop me from attending the first meeting of my local Toastmasters chapter. The meeting was in the basement of a church and I was extremely nervous. All I kept thinking was, "Don't call on me" or worse yet that I'd have to stand up and introduce myself!" The good news is that none of those things happened. I could have saved myself a ton of worry if I had *expected* things to go smoothly and to be welcomed by the group. In general, Toastmasters groups are supportive and designed for individuals to set their own pace with regard to participation. And that's exactly what I did: attended meetings, observed, and made small talk until I was comfortable and ready to participate.

My very first meeting was a teachable moment for me. After a number of weeks, I realized that much of the fear and anxiety that we create around public speaking is self-induced, "What if this happens? What if that happens? What if I pass out? What if my fly is open? What if I have something between my teeth? What if I embarrass myself?" The self-induced anxiety is very real and in many instance you don't even know you're creating it. When others in the group got up to give a speech, I often felt their anxiety in my own body. How could this be? Even though I thought I had little or no control over my physical symptoms, it wasn't long before I learned that it was yours truly who was causing many of my physical symptoms: shallow breathing, flushed cheeks, and muscle tension. I had become so proficient at creating my own anxiety which had been a part of my routine for so many years, that it never occurred to me I was the one in charge of it. Once you recognize that the source of your anxiety is you, the next logical question is how to stop.

Free resources at http://www.publicspeakingsimple.com/

There are a number of techniques that can alleviate your anxiety, which I'll cover throughout this guide. However, before going down that path you must first realize that *you are the cause of your anxiety* and fear of public speaking. When I say this most people who are struggling with public speaking cringe or shut down, as I did at first. It's a hard pill to swallow. I recall thinking to myself, "I'm powerless. I can't control my heart from racing" and "I'm not creating my fear of public speaking, I've always had it!" Nevertheless, the sooner you take 100 percent responsibility for your own fear, the sooner you become empowered to deal with it. Think of it this way: If something outside of you were responsible for your anxiety how could you ever hope to control it - you'd have identify it, constantly keep it in check, and ward against it. This would be difficult, if not impossible, because any situation could potentially cause anxiety. The sooner you realize where the anxiety is actually coming from, the faster you can overcome your fear.

What most people don't tell you about anxiety

It took me many years to learn this but the best way to deal with anxiety is to recognize it without focusing on it. This may be difficult to grasp, but essentially you don't want to get emotionally involved with your anxiety, simply recognize *it*. By keeping anxiety separate, something you don't have to control, you gain tremendous power over it. Don't let anxiety coax you into a battle. When you focus on anxious feelings and get emotionally involved, that's when things go sour. Recognize symptoms of anxiety by calling it out, identifying *it* for what it is, but don't go toe to toe - it's a losing battle and one you can choose to avoid.

An example of this is when I became consciously aware of the physical symptoms I had like a racing heart beat before each presentation. In the past I would feel my heart beating out of my chest and start to jump into a downward spiral of negative

Free resources at http://www.publicspeakingsimple.com/

talk. Now, if I experience any physical symptoms, I either ignore them completely or say something like, "my heart is racing, that's interesting" Again, the point is that it's okay to experience any physical symptom, just don't jump on the bandwagon with negative self-talk or make it your only focus. This gets easier with time but can be a major shifting point for those who want to lessen their anxiety but don't yet have control of certain physical reactions.

Anxiety isn't entirely a bad thing. I've learned that you never alleviate your anxiety 100 percent. Being nervous is OK—it is part of the puzzle, a natural reaction to standing up in front of others where all eyes are upon you. If you weren't nervous, I'd question whether you were taking your presentation seriously. The key is to accept the healthy part of your anxiety and re-label it as something positive. I'll show you how to do this in greater detail so what you currently label anxiety no longer exists.

One person who really convinced me that anxiety didn't have to get the last word was a man I met while attending Toastmasters. Elliot, who was the MC, generally started each of the meetings. He was clearly one of the best public speakers I had ever met, and it was no surprise that he had command of the entire audience. He exuded such confidence, yet he didn't come off as being arrogant or unapproachable. I guess you could say that he was a likeable guy. After asking a few people about Elliot's background, I was surprised to find out he hadn't always been that way. In fact, for most of his life, Elliot had been ridiculed and teased because of a pronounced stutter. It wasn't until he was in his mid-forties that he discovered Toastmasters and conquered his biggest obstacle, regaining his confidence and transforming his life. How did he do it? When I spoke with him one on one, Elliot explained that it was a combination of believing he could make a change and developing specific skills that allowed him to speak like a pro. By seeing others overcome the same challenges Elliot slowly started to believe in himself. "If they can do it, so can I," he thought. This proved to be one of the most powerful steps in his

Free resources at http://www.publicspeakingsimple.com/

transformation. Once he added specific skills, including effective breathing and preparation, he was well on his way to becoming a powerful speaker and feeling much more comfortable in front of any audience.

There are many more stories like this one, and new ones are being created every day. People find ways to overcome their speaking challenges and accomplish their goals. I feel fortunate to have overcome the fear of public speaking, and it all started with an eagerness to change. If you share that eagerness, you will find your solution in the pages ahead.

The *TODAY Show*

The more time that I dedicated to improving my speaking skills, the more progress I made. Assimilating everything I learned from my mentor, Toastmasters, and personal observations of people presenting in both small settings and on a large stage took many months. The more I started applying a number of these principals to my own presentations in front of small and large groups. The more time spent applying skills the easier presenting became. In time, I actually found myself enjoying the effectiveness of my presentations and sharing my knowledge with others. I would even seek out more opportunities to present, anytime, anywhere. It sounds strange to anyone who has an acute fear of public speaking or is currently struggling with their speaking ability, but presenting to others became virtually effortless.

One of the keys to success for me was volunteering for opportunities to speak first and speak often, no matter how uncomfortable I felt. By putting myself out there and developing my skills, I encountered new opportunities to further enhance my abilities…and just in time.

Within two years of conquering my fear, I was given the opportunity to speak on the *TODAY Show* in front of an

Free resources at http://www.publicspeakingsimple.com/

audience of more than six million people. I was at a crossroads. Was I truly ready to take on this life-changing opportunity? Speaking in front of an audience is one thing but being on a nationally televised show is completely something else. Once the initial shock passed over me, my mind moved towards gratitude. It wasn't long before I realized that all of the work invested to build my skills had prepared me for this moment to come. It was the next step in my journey and a proving ground for the skills I'm sharing with you in this book.

The opportunity came about so quickly. A call came in from our company's public relations agency and we had only three days to prepare. Since I had been developing my speaking skills, we were able to use the available time to develop the content knowledge I'd need for the interview. I spent a couple of days with our product team and almost a full day in media training. What I learned in those few days greatly enhanced my public speaking skills and became the source of a number of techniques I'll be sharing with you on how to overcome anxiety and present with confidence.

When I showed up at the studio, there was a lot to take in. This was certainly a new experience for me and I could have easily fallen back into bad behaviors such as self-doubt, anxiety, and fear. However, doing so wasn't really an option. Many people were counting on me to successfully deliver a message and in a few short moments it would all be over. I knew I didn't have the luxury of caving in to anxiety. I was escorted to a seat in the studio in pitch darkness. It seemed like just a few moments before hearing someone count "Three...two..." and the lights came on instantly. My heartbeat sped as the fact that we were broadcasting live sank in. This was it—the moment I had been preparing for, and I was ready.

There's no doubt that I felt a mixture of emotions at that moment: excitement, anxiousness, and gratitude all racing through me at the same time. I could feel the adrenaline in my body and I remembered how it used to control me. Within a few

Free resources at http://www.publicspeakingsimple.com/

short minutes I was generally at ease and fully engaged in the interview. Matt Lauer was a great host and the interview was a huge success for everyone involved. Thinking back to that moment leaves me grateful for the opportunity and humbled by the journey that helped me get there. Looking at the recording of that day there are certainly aspects of the interview I would have changed—some things I would have said differently—but overall it's quite a feat. For a guy who started out as a nervous kid virtually paralyzed by reading out loud in grade school to participating in a successful interview on the *TODAY Show*—I determined that my fear had been conquered.

After the interview, I found still more reason to believe that anyone can become a public speaker. When we finished the interview Matt Lauer had a short break and actually engaged in a little chitchat with me. He proved to be a normal guy and quite personable. As I was on my way out of the studio, in came Katie Couric, who stopped, shook my hand, and said, "Thank you for coming to the *TODAY Show*." You could have knocked me over with a feather. Katie Couric, the woman I had watched on the *TODAY Show* for nearly a decade, was thanking me for appearing on one of the most popular morning shows of all time! In that instant, I learned that much of the fear we create is self-induced. I so often feared my audience, the critics, my superiors, and, of course, these larger-than-life personalities, but the reality is they are just like you and me. They also appreciate the time and effort you've put into your presentation. We often don't give ourselves enough credit for the effort we make or realize how much time public speakers have dedicated to overcoming fear.

The reality is that if I hadn't learned the valuable lessons of believing in myself and some simple strategies of effective public speaking, I would never have done it. I would never have developed the confidence in my own abilities to speak publicly or successfully navigate a television interview. My goal for you is to conquer your fear, improve your comfort level, and to never, ever, let the anxiety of speaking in front of others hold you back. Effective public speaking can and will have an impact

Free resources at http://www.publicspeakingsimple.com/

on both your personal and professional life. Those who master the art of speaking in front of others go through life with fewer limitations than those who do not. Congratulations on starting this journey—you'll be glad you did.

Conquering your fear

Interestingly enough, some people are great when conversing one-on-one but as soon as they have to stand up in front of an audience, they transform into anxiety-ridden neophytes. This common problem can be addressed with the right mind-set and effective public speaking strategies.

From my perspective, public speaking simply means speaking to a group larger than one. Often we view speaking situations (one-on-one vs. one-to-many) as entirely different but in reality they share many similarities. Whether you're speaking to one person or more, you still need to speak loudly enough to be heard, feel confident, and say something of value. You need to make eye contact with one person at a time. And you need to present a clear idea or concept in a fairly articulate manner. The only difference is a small increase in complexity when reaching more than one person with your message. Yes, it's more complex to make eye contact with five hundred people in a room. (We'll look at how to give the impression of eye contact in larger groups later.) And it takes more practice to make your voice carry thirty feet than three feet. But you'll still find many similarities between speaking situations in which you are comfortable and those in which you are currently uncomfortable. The key is to focus on the similarities, not the differences. Doing so enables you to bring the same level of confidence and comfort into new speaking situations.

As you gain experience and focus on the aspects of speaking that you know, it becomes easier to address situations that cause anxiety. These uneasy feelings more can come from a lack of confidence or a negative experience you had in the

Free resources at http://www.publicspeakingsimple.com/

past. Regardless of what is causing your anxiety, there are proven strategies to get beyond these obstacles and speak with confidence. It all begins with some basic ideas and beliefs that you can adopt starting today.

1. Believe it's possible. Conquering the fear and anxiety associated with public speaking is possible only for those who *believe* it's possible. The good news is that just by reading this book you believe it is possible deep within you. That's all you need to start down the path to developing confidence in yourself and the ability to speak with certainty. Regardless of your previous experience, effective public speaking is within your reach. How can you be sure? Because you see other people speaking with ease and confidence every day and many of them struggled for a lot longer than you have.

The next question you should be asking yourself is how to strengthen your belief. How can you change your current mind-set so you not only see yourself as a confident speaker but start to act on your newfound belief? The good news is that changing your belief system is relatively simple. It takes a little time and definiteness of purpose, but before long you'll experience a transformation in beliefs. I've learned a couple of simple techniques I'm going to share with you now to start the process of developing a strong belief in your ability to take on the characteristics of a strong public speaker. These techniques are easy to implement but require patience and a little bit of effort:

- Expose yourself to live presentations and listen to speakers (video or audio) on a daily basis.

- See yourself, in your mind's eye, giving a strong presentation.

By seeking out and attending as many presentations as you can—live or online—you'll actually start becoming more

Free resources at http://www.publicspeakingsimple.com/

comfortable with the whole idea of giving a presentation. If you don't have access to live speakers on a regular basis, start watching videos of well-known speakers like Anthony Robbins, Wayne Dyer, Zig Ziglar, Les Brown, and others on YouTube for just fifteen minutes a day. After watching and listening to some of the best presenters, you will become much more comfortable in a speaker-like setting. In fact, you'll probably start saying things like, "I can do that" or "This doesn't look so difficult" after a short while.

When you first begin watching presentations, you may feel some anxiety even though you are not the person presenting. This is natural. Be mindful of your internal dialog. If you catch yourself thinking things like "I can't do this" or "I'll never be as good as that speaker," then you need to change your internal dialogue. Replace your negative statements with more positive ones like "I can become an effective public speaker" or "Listening to these speakers will help me improve." Write the statements down on a few index cards and post them all over your home, in your car, and in your office. Having a positive internal dialogue is one of the fastest ways to improve self-talk and develop your belief, but it takes repetition and constant exposure.

As you listen to others speaking, watch how they manage their anxiety. Do they appear outwardly nervous when they speak? Do you notice inflections in their voice? Are there certain things they say or do that you might be able to apply to your own presentations to mitigate anxiety? Do you notice speakers moving throughout the audience or using visual aids? The more speakers you are exposed to the easier it becomes to identify winning strategies that can dramatically improve your own presentations. As you gain more exposure to speakers of all types, anxiety lessens and you become comfortable with various speaking styles. After exposing yourself to a variety of speakers you'll likely identify strategies and styles that work for you.

Free resources at http://www.publicspeakingsimple.com/

Take every opportunity you can to view speakers and presentations either live or via YouTube and other social media websites. I would argue that if you were to attend one hundred hours of presentations, you'd be a completely different person —not only from the content you'd assimilate but through the exposure to so many different presentations. If a hundred hours seems like an unrealistic goal, start with ten hours or even just three hours of exposure. Work your way up and get as much experience as you can long before you ever have to present on your own or make you next speech. This first step takes hardly any courage, yet it starts diminishing the fear without any battle on your part.

When I wanted to start improving my public speaking skills I listened to some of the great presenters and motivational speakers, including Tony Robbins, Brian Tracy, and Napoleon Hill. I even attended a number of live sessions for a hefty fee to see some of these "gurus" present, though the recordings were extremely helpful too. These speakers were so genuine and engaging that I found myself repeating many of their catch phrases and mannerisms in my own presentations. In fact, hearing them say things repeatedly made me both proficient in articulating specific ideas I learned from them and confident in my ability to do so. With the pervasiveness of audio and video, watching presenters is easier than ever, and I strongly recommend that you listen to as many speakers as you can on a regular basis. However, don't skip live presentations when you can attend them. There are a number of strategies and nuances to a live presentation that you just can't get by watching a video.

Once you're underway watching and listening to presentations on a regular basis, the next step is vital for changing your belief system – seeing yourself, in your mind's eye, confidently and effectively presenting to others. The exposure to other speakers will help you begin to formulate an image of what a good speaker looks like, sounds like, and acts like. This is why I recommend lots of exposure to many presentations before introducing this step of visualization.

Free resources at http://www.publicspeakingsimple.com/

While the thought of creating an image of yourself feeling comfortable speaking in front of others may be difficult at first, stick with it. As long as you're persistent and practice the technique daily, even if for only a few minutes per day, you'll experience the tremendous benefits associated with visualization. If you're new to visualization, you may have some doubts about this age-old technique, but it works. One commonality among powerful public speakers is their ability to see themselves delivering great presentations. Follow these strategies to get started with the process of visualization:

- Put yourself into a relaxed state by sitting or lying in a comfortable position, closing your eyes, and breathing slowly. You may even want to slowly count backwards from thirty as you breathe in and breathe out. Also consider a relaxation playlist to help put your mind at ease.

- Once you are relaxed, imagine yourself presenting in front of a small audience at first. Maybe you're in a room with your friends showing them something new you bought and explaining how it works. The setting could be around the kitchen table, in a meeting room, or some other small venue. Over time, you're going to build on the image, adding friends, acquaintances, and even moving to larger rooms and presenting in front of larger audiences.

- Repeat this process each night as you begin to fall asleep. See and feel yourself as a confident speaker giving an effective presentation. See your audience clapping, nodding, celebrating what you have to share, and feel their support. Getting emotionally involved with the idea is the key to visualization success.

- Do this visual exercise every night for a month, building larger audiences in your mind as you are able. With each mental rehearsal, your visualization skills will improve and you'll be amazed at how much better you feel at the thought of giving a presentation.

Free resources at http://www.publicspeakingsimple.com/

This one technique, visualization, has helped me to significantly reduce my stress and build my confidence. As I noted earlier, it may be difficult or awkward at first, especially if you're new to visualization. Tell yourself that it's OK if you can't see images clearly or if you find it difficult to focus on your mental presentations and keep going. The goal is progress, not perfection. It took me some time to get comfortable with the visualization process, but the results have been amazing. The only way to fail at this exercise is to stop too soon. I have met many people who get off track by trying it for a few days or a week at most and saying, "It doesn't work." Your anxiety wasn't created in a week, and, until there's a magic pill, it won't go away in a week either. However, by exposing yourself to presenters and using visualization, it will start to diminish—ultimately disappearing. But you have to make the effort.

I've found that one of the best times to practice this technique is when you close your eyes at night. You're usually thinking about something when you put your head on the pillow, so why not change the pictures in your mind from the meeting you have with your boss the next day to yourself giving a great presentation to others? I also apply the technique first thing in the morning. Find a time that works for you. The key is to continue practicing the technique until it's part of your every-day routine.

With these two techniques, you'll be well down the path to becoming an effective public speaker. It's highly likely that you will already see a reduction in your speech-induced anxiety. To reduce your anxiety even more, you will use a variety of techniques that strengthen your belief in yourself and your abilities. I know the mere thought of addressing your anxiety may actually make you anxious. Therefore we need to reframe the way we think about anxiety so it becomes much less overwhelming.

Free resources at http://www.publicspeakingsimple.com/

2. Reframe your anxiety. After having the fortune of talking to many powerful speakers, I learned that very rarely, if ever, do they talk about "fear" or "anxiety." In fact, those words are not even part of their regular vocabulary. Could it be possible that to eliminate these unwanted emotions all you have to do is remove them from your vocabulary? Surprisingly the answer is yes, and it appears to be a common practice among many of today's most effective speakers. I personally used this technique to eliminate much of my fear, and I no longer talk about anxiety when referring to my feelings before giving speeches. Let me explain how this works and how you can apply the technique immediately to put you more at ease.

Prior to giving a presentation, you are going to feel something—anxiety, nervousness, discomfort. To overcome these feelings, you need to do two things. The first is to accept them—don't try to eliminate what you're feeling or get emotionally involved with them. I heard a great quote once that still rings true today: "What you resist persists." Accept your feelings regardless of what they may be, and let them wash over you. In other words, let go. Don't waste your energy trying to fight them. The more you focus on or fight them, the more intense they become.

Instead of focusing on the discomfort acknowledge that you're feeling anxious and be OK with that. Anxiety is a good thing because it keeps us alert. Don't try to control these feelings; simply accept them for what they are. When I began accepting my anxiety and stopped beating myself up because of it, my internal dialogue went from "I'm so anxious, I could die" to "I'm feeling anxious right now and that's OK." By focusing on your internal dialogue, you are going to address this uncomfortable feeling in a new way and minimize its intensity. As you notice anxiety starting to build, use phrases like the one above or "This anxiety is natural," "I'm OK with my anxiety," or "Everyone gets nervous before a presentation," or "The feelings I'm having are no big deal."

Free resources at http://www.publicspeakingsimple.com/

Next you need to re-label your anxiety. As mentioned previously, powerful speakers don't use the word "anxiety." I'd actually go so far as to say that I never want you to use the word "anxiety" when referring to public speaking in any capacity. Instead, re-label your feelings as "excitement." That's right—"excitement." Similar to a rock band getting pumped up before going on stage or a sports team ready to take the field, excitement is the emotion we're looking for. Using a new label evokes a new feeling, new emotion. Instead of telling yourself that you are feeling anxious, tell yourself that you're feeling excited, pumped up, jazzed, confident, ready to go! This one fundamental change will build your enthusiasm, excitement, and confidence. Most importantly, it lessons your anxiety. Use this technique each time those old feelings come up. Remember that repetition is essential for this to be truly effective.

Excitement is an essential element for sharing what you know with your audience. If you're not excited about the material you're presenting, how can anyone else get excited about it? This is what today's most speakers understand above all else. They're genuinely excited about sharing what they know with their audience and giving something of value to them. When you help others learn something through a speech or presentation, you're making a difference. Don't underestimate the value of what you have to offer. You're helping others and that's something to get excited about. Reframing your anxiety as excitement is an essential skill, not only for public speaking but for many of life's situations.

It's important to note that as you begin to visualize and reframe your anxiety as excitement, you may experience a lag. A lag means that as you're preparing yourself to improve, you continue to feel a good deal of uneasiness. This is because your body hasn't necessarily caught up with your brain. Permanent change requires practice and repetition. Be patient with yourself, and look for small improvements in your self-talk and the de-escalation of physical symptoms. Realize that you many initially have to feel the fear and go through the

Free resources at http://www.publicspeakingsimple.com/

presentation anyway until your discomfort is greatly reduced or eliminated altogether.

3. Proper breathing. One of the reasons that people experience anxiety is because of the way they label their feelings. Another cause is physical in the form of shortness of breath—a symptom and a cause of anxiety. When people experience shortness of breath or shallow breathing, they often start saying things like "I can't breathe." This naturally causes more panic, and the vicious cycle begins. I know because I used to live it before every single presentation. However, unless you're presenting underwater, you're never in a situation where you can't breathe. In fact if you really couldn't breathe, your body is smart enough to pass out to ensure that you go back to breathing naturally. So the good news is that our natural programming has us covered. Don't ever worry about passing out again: it's actually a method of survival. Instead, focus on changing your breathing and relabeling your feelings to something more positive. If you're worried about passing out during a presentation, I'd put that fear aside as well. There's a .001% chance of you passing out. Change your-self talk. You're part of the 99.999% who doesn't have to worry about it.

The idea of passing out was something that I had to deal with. My anxiety and fear was so intense that as soon as I experienced shortness of breath, I assumed the next step was passing out. In reality, there are a few other things that would happen before you actually lose consciousness. I'm not saying this to be funny but to stress how unlikely it is that "passing out" would ever happen to you or another presenter you happen to be watching – it's a fallacy. And, if by some sort of weird twist of fate you did pass out, you'd have plenty of people to come to your aid. You certainly wouldn't be the first person on the planet to fall over in the presence of others – so put it out of your mind, relax, and focus on the positive.

Free resources at http://www.publicspeakingsimple.com/

Personally however, one of the things I had to work on was proper breathing. Proper breathing is when you inhale through your nose and out through your mouth via your diaphragm, which is right behind your belly button. Shortness of breath generally happens when you're breathing through just your mouth and chest. The way I changed this automatic reaction was through practice. Just like when you are using visualization, put yourself in a relaxed state. Count backward from thirty if you're having trouble. Place one hand over your belly button and one hand on your chest. Practice the technique of slowly breathing through your nose and out through your mouth. Do you feel your diaphragm expanding? The hand on your belly should rise and the hand on your chest should remain still. Over time this becomes your natural state, but you must practice. Don't expect to magically start breathing in a different way; you must create a new history through practice.

Changing the physical aspects of breathing also changes what you experience. Best of all, as the process becomes natural you won't have to give thought or effort to this calming technique. As you build your breathing skills, you'll find yourself in a more relaxed state – closer to hanging out with a friend as opposed to what you might feel walking up to a complete stranger at a bar. Physically you'll experience some changes as well such as a lack of dizziness, less tension in your body, and a feeling of calm.

4. Do it anyway. Exposure, visualization, transforming fear to excitement, and breathing properly will take you far, but some physical symptoms of anxiety may still remain. As I went through this process, even though I was labeling my feelings as excitement instead of anxiety, my body was telling me a different story. Determined to succeed, I pushed forward anyway.

Free resources at http://www.publicspeakingsimple.com/

Your mind works much more quickly than your body which takes time to realize all of the benefits associated with a new way of thinking. Your body is sending you false signals, and your job is to accept and overcome these false signals. Given that, you must accept that you're going to experience some initial discomfort and push forward through it. It will become much easier in a short period of time. It takes conscious effort to think your way through the anxiety, but it can be done. While one of your goals is to mitigate the symptoms associated with anxiety (through the steps mentioned earlier), your second goal is to increase your tolerance for them. This means doing it anyway, despite any feelings of discomfort.

Managing these feelings can be compared to that of driving a car into a skid. Living in the Northeast, I've had my share of days driving in the snow. When traveling in bad weather, it's inevitable that at some point your car will skid. As someone who's been driving for a long time, I've learned the valuable lesson of always looking in the direction I want my car to go, not where I'm headed against my will. However, this isn't a natural tendency for most drivers. When entering a skid, most people look to where they don't want to go—a street sign, over the curb, or into another car. Unfortunately, focusing on where you *don't* want to go often ends badly. The good news is that when you get the hang of turning your head in the direction you want the car to go, part way into the skid the wheels will grip and the car turns in the proper direction. Essentially, the car takes a moment to catch up to your mental and physical reaction to the skid. Improving your public speaking and minimizing anxiety works the same way. Give it time and focus on where you want to go and the proper results will follow.

As I personally applied each of the techniques I just shared with you, my overall mental disposition began to improve. Through a long process of trial and error, it was clear that the strategies of exposure to lots of presentations both live and recorded, relabeling negative emotions into positive ones, visualization, proper breathing, and moving forward despite having some physical symptoms of anxiety still remain. In

Free resources at http://www.publicspeakingsimple.com/

addition to learning through my own experience I began to integrate strategies from other speakers to hone my skills. In the next section I share some of the most effective techniques I've learned from others who were at the top of their game and elevated my understanding of becoming a great presenter.

Free resources at http://www.publicspeakingsimple.com/

Chapter 2

Powerful Lessons from Effective Speakers

Free resources at http://www.publicspeakingsimple.com/

A number of years ago while attending an executive event, I had the opportunity to hear Rudy Giuliani, the former Mayor of New York City, speak in person. Giuliani is applauded as one of the most influential mayors of all time for the Big Apple, and many see him as an icon—someone who turned around an ailing city and improved day to day living in New York. The company I worked for at the time hosted an executive retreat every year to review the previous year's performance and discuss strategies for future growth and expansion. It would bring in a number of industry leaders or a headline presenter who aligned with the vision of our company and goals. As a big fan of the former New York City mayor I was incredibly excited to hear him speak and share some of his most effective techniques for influencing change. What I didn't realize at the time was that many of his techniques would become my most effective public speaking strategies too.

Even though Rudy Giuliani's presentation was more than a decade ago, many of his lessons are still with me and were essential for developing into an effective speaker. One of those lessons came from his experience as the attorney general, which involved giving oral presentations on a daily basis. One thing that attorneys do well is prepare for arguments and persuade their audience to a particular point of view. It became apparent that the ability to have this impact on others doesn't happen by chance; it is based on adequate preparation and the application of specific strategies.

One strategy in particular was probably the most significant for helping me overcome much of my anxiety and move from simply making a presentation to becoming a bona fide speaker – getting paid to present.

The rule of four. Mr. Giuliani spoke of his "rule of four" which served as a guide for preparation. The rule suggested that for every hour of oral arguments he anticipated presenting in the courtroom, he rehearsed for four hours. Why four hours? I can

Free resources at http://www.publicspeakingsimple.com/

tell you as someone who's applied this rule every time I prepare for a speech, that you are not only using that time to refine your presentation, but also plan for any potential issue you might encounter.

Whether you're preparing for the courtroom, boardroom, or meeting room, adequate preparation is the key to success. When you take the time to practice, rehearse, practice again, think through possible questions your audience may ask you, and any issues associated with what you're saying and how you're saying it, you build confidence in your public speaking abilities. More importantly, you position yourself to handle just about anything that comes your way. Even if you're asked a question by the audience you haven't rehearsed for, you've probably thought about something similar during your four hours of rehearsal which will help you respond. Keep in mind that actual rehearsal doesn't include the time it takes you to write your presentation or put together a power point.

After learning about this technique, I began using it and immediately saw the impact. Before that, no one had given me a guideline on preparation or even stressed its importance. The rule of 4 provides significant benefits that extend beyond the presentation itself and are too numerous to count. Not only was my speaking smoother with more extensive preparation, but I discovered more confidence in address any and all issues associated with my presentation, whether it was dealing with different personalities in the room, a projector that didn't work, or a slide presentation I didn't have access too. Preparation following the four-to-one ratio elevates your ability to navigate effectively when confronted with the unexpected. I never do a planned presentation without adequate preparation anymore because it exponentially improves my results and helps me feel much more confident and relaxed.

Only doing a 15 minute presentation? Use the same ratio prescribed by the "Rule of 4", prepare for 60 minutes. How about a thirty-minute webinar? Prepare for at least two hours.

Free resources at http://www.publicspeakingsimple.com/

Again, keep in mind this time is not for creating your slides or writing your notes. Thirty minutes of rehearsal means spending thirty minutes of time actually talking—going through your presentation over and over again.

Rehearsing builds confidence, subject matter expertise, and the ability to think well on your feet. Without adequate practice I guarantee that you'll feel anxious and unprepared. Now that you have a specific plan for how long you should prepare for each of your presentations, apply the rule to any type of presentation or speech you may be giving. It elevates your results and builds confidence like nothing else.

Mirror, mirror. Another technique I learned from powerful speakers is called "mirror, mirror." My mentor had me use this method to ease my anxiety when in front of others and improve my body language. Once I practiced enough, the technique became second nature and is now another resource I use for every presentation. It has without a doubt proved to be one of the best techniques in my arsenal for public speaking. Not only is it incredibly simple to implement but also has lasting results.

After you've written your presentation, rehearse while standing in front of a mirror. It's ideal if you have a full-length mirror in which you can see your whole body, but any mirror will do. When you rehearse, look at yourself casually and make eye contact with your reflection. This may seem a bit awkward at first but there are a number of reasons why this technique is so effective.

The first reason you want to practice this way is because you see exactly what the audience sees. There's no guessing or confusion about what things look like from their vantage point. The question of what the audience sees is often a source of anxiety without our even knowing it. We get nervous about others seeing our faults, real or imagined. When you look

Free resources at http://www.publicspeakingsimple.com/

yourself in the eye, you start becoming more comfortable with what the audience is actually seeing.

The second reason is that you're going to get more comfortable in your own skin. Seeing yourself delivering your presentation puts you at ease and builds confidence—something I was really lacking. It may take some time to get used to seeing your reflection in the mirror but doing so is essential for removing questions about your own abilities. As you spend time with yourself, delivering your presentation over and over again, your confidence rises. Having all eyes upon you won't be as threatening as it may have been in the past because you now know exactly what the audience is seeing and feel better about yourself—wonderful you.

As I worked on improving my public speaking skills with this technique, using a mirror was ideal for refining my gestures and facial expressions. For example, after seeing myself present for the first time, I realized I needed to practice some physical changes, such as smiling more, standing up straight, and changing my stance. Making these changes didn't come naturally but over time, I improved. Without standing in front of a mirror, identifying these areas for improvement would have been difficult. When you begin practicing in front of a mirror, look at the things you're not happy with as an opportunity for enhancing your presentation skills.

After initially learning about this technique, I was really excited to give it a try. Starting small, I began practicing in front of my bathroom mirror where I could only see my facial expressions. Over time, as I got comfortable using the mirror, mirror technique, and moving to a full-length mirror provided me with even more feedback on my presentation style. Don't be afraid to start small and work your way up. This technique helps you improve in virtually every way when it comes to public speaking and can grow in nuance as your skills advance. It's also the stepping-stone to your next technique.

Free resources at http://www.publicspeakingsimple.com/

Videotaping. I look funny. At least that was my first reaction to seeing myself present to a live audience. Truthfully, I wouldn't have had such a difficult time watching the playback if I had been a better speaker at the time. Many concerns surfaced in watching that video, and it was a bit discouraging until I recognized the recording as an opportunity to identify areas for improvement. At the time of the recording, I was still in the process of overcoming my fear of public speaking and really didn't have a good handle on things—that was clear. My presentation was choppy at best and I was extremely nervous (aka excited). It was clear that I didn't have a firm grasp on the material and it showed. "Um" seemed to interject itself into virtually every pause and my movements were nothing short of awkward. It's difficult to imagine what the audience thought about my speech but having everything captured on video tape gave me a unique opportunity to learn about my own behaviors on stage.

As difficult as it was to watch the presentation (over and over again), it really was one of the best ways to learn what I did well and what needed improvement. Without it, I don't think I'd have such a clear idea of what aspects of development to focus on. I certainly wouldn't have known how necessary the changes were. Now that video cameras are readily available on mobile phones, cameras, webcams, tablets, and more, finding a way to record your presentation shouldn't be difficult.

Using video to critique is nothing new. When I was learning to play golf, I paid for a few lessons from a golf professional. What was the first thing he did? You guessed it: he videotaped my swing. At first I thought, what's the point? He already knows I'm awful I thought to myself. Why record a really bad swing? But the purpose of the recording was not for the golf pro. I'm sure he saw what was wrong with me in the first few seconds of my picking up a golf club. Rather, his goal was to show *me* my swing and compare it to a professional's golf swing. Once he was done videotaping, we went inside and he ran the video on a split screen. One-half of the monitor showed my swing, and the other half showed that of a pro. It made for a stark contrast.

Free resources at http://www.publicspeakingsimple.com/

Most importantly, I could see for myself what I was doing wrong. It is one thing for someone to tell you what you're doing wrong and another to see it with your very own eyes!

Videotaping my golf swing saved me many hours of studying how to improve on the golf course. Instead of focusing on the negatives, it had me focusing on the perfect swing and making the necessary adjustments to be more aligned with the best swing possible. This is the goal of using a video recording of your presentations. When you see yourself during playback, focus on making changes that bring you closer to your ideal as a confident, well-spoken presenter.

If you're recording a speech at home or live, see it as an opportunity to identify both strengths and weaknesses. Remember, you're not doing this to beat yourself up. Always focus on what's working well and what can be improved. As you build on your strengths and address weaknesses, you'll notice a significant transformation in your poise, polish, and level of comfort in front of an audience.

Come back to this technique again and again. Improving your public speaking is not a one-time event. I still critique my presentations using video, even though I've spent plenty of time practicing my trade; there's always more to fine-tune and improve.

Starting small. Due to my high level of anxiety, my first mentor had me practice my presentations in front of him. After a while, he started bringing a couple of his friends over to listen as well. I remember being in his apartment, repeating the same presentation over and over again. I don't even know if his buddies were truly listening but it certainly got me comfortable presenting in front of others and thoroughly knowledgeable about my subject matter.

Free resources at http://www.publicspeakingsimple.com/

This technique may seem obvious especially if you're still uncomfortable presenting in front of a group, large or small. However, even when asked to do large presentations, I ask that you start small. My mentor never detailed this strategy for me, but he didn't have to. Through the process of presenting in front of a mirror, then in front of him, then again in front of a group of friends, he was teaching me a valuable lesson—start small and work your way up.

Take for an example the marketing executive who's been asked to give a large presentation. His boss, the chief marketing officer, informs him that the presentation will take place at the company meeting in front of five hundred executives, managers, and employees. This marketing executive has an acute fear of public speaking and has to figure out how to pull off the seemingly impossible task of doing such a significant presentation to such a large group. In addition to the using the before mentioned techniques, he needs to start small.

This executive, let's call him Bob, decides that any attempt to get out of the presentation can only work against him and his career so he decides the only option is to push forward despite his apparent anxiety. He speaks to his boss and admits that he's incredibly nervous about presenting to this group. Understanding Bob's concern, the boss suggests presenting together. Bob believes that working in partnership should ease the stress of a solo presentation, but it still requires him to stand up in front of a large audience. Although a partner presentation may seem less stressful, Bob will have to prepare in much the same way he would without the help of a partner. To get ready for the presentation, he chooses to start small and work his way up to giving a presentation to a larger audience.

After rehearsing in front of the mirror and getting comfortable with his portion of the presentation, Bob asks to present to a couple of his close friends at the company. They agree to listen and after doing so provide some really helpful feedback. Bob is

Free resources at http://www.publicspeakingsimple.com/

nervous even in front of this small group but found that the longer he presented the more comfortable he became. Once Bob has refined his presentation and rehearsed some more, he presents to his marketing department. Having these presentations under his belt gives him the confidence to face an even larger audience. After presenting to the marketing department, he does a webinar for his company division, sharing his findings and taking some questions and answers from the audience. In a short period of time, Bob has not only worked his way up to larger and larger audiences, he's also rehearsed his presentation and refined it multiple times. It's likely he's even met the rule of four at this point.

Even if you only have a couple of days to prepare, you can always find an audience to rehearse in front of. People genuinely want you to succeed and there's no shame in asking for help or finding someone who can listen to your presentation. If you can't find an actual person, present to your dog, cat, or fish. The goal is to improve your ability to present to others, no matter who they happen to be.

As I shared earlier in this book, I never would have been able to get through my *TODAY Show* interview without the benefit of starting small and working my way up to larger and larger audiences. Although speaking on television is a different experience all together, having multiple rehearsals under my belt made a significant difference. I recall being very excited at the start of the interview and getting comfortable after I started focusing on the content and the questions. This was largely due to my preparing as for any other speech, which meant frequent rehearsal, feedback from smaller audiences, and refinement.

Effective public speaking is like building a muscle. You can't show up at the gym for the first time and bench press 350 pounds. It starts with lifting a small weight, adding more each time you do the exercise, building strength. Start with the smallest audience possible (one). Face yourself in the mirror

Free resources at http://www.publicspeakingsimple.com/

and begin to rehearse your presentation. Once you're comfortable presenting to yourself, add another. Expand your audience to coworkers, friends, and larger audiences. In no time at all, you'll be lifting more public speaking "weight" than you ever imagined and it will begin coming naturally.

Repetition

An effective presentation is greatly enhanced with adequate practice. This is one thing my mentor kept drilling into my head. It certainly reached the point of annoyance, but keep in mind that you are not only practicing the material itself but also preparing for anything that may come your way while you give a speech. Expect the unexpected, and know that the best remedy for surprises is practice and repetition.

When I was in business development a number of years ago, an executive from the parent company asked me to accompany him on a presentation to a very large potential client. Knowing how large the potential business opportunity was only made me more nervous about the upcoming meeting but there was no escaping the inevitable. With my newfound understanding of adequate preparation, I decided to put in the necessary effort to ensure a flawless presentation—and I'm glad I did. Over a period of many days I rehearsed in the mirror, in the car, in front of colleagues, and in front of anyone else who would listen, covering the material over and over again. As I prepared for the meeting I began to think about all of the things that were in my control and those that weren't. For instance, I realized that although my PowerPoint presentation was finely tuned, there could be technical difficulties, so I should bring my own computer and projector. I also realized how important the slides were to my presentation and burned a backup to a flash drive and printed out hard copies for my audience. I wouldn't have considered any of these preparations if I hadn't spent the time thinking through the presentation and rehearsing. You might

Free resources at http://www.publicspeakingsimple.com/

notice that none of these potential issues had anything to do with the content but rather the presentation itself. Through repetition I began to account for multiple aspects of the meeting.

After we arrived at the client's site, my partner and I were brought to the meeting room. Already waiting for us was a room of executives seated around a large table. After finding our seats and receiving a quick introduction, we were told that we had fifteen minutes to present, not the hour we had been promised before arriving. I quickly reached into my back and pulled out my computer. The executive across the table said, "We don't have a projector."

"No problem, I brought my own," I said.

After my computer booted, I clicked on my PowerPoint and nothing happened, it wouldn't start. Instead of panicking, I put in my flash drive and began the presentation. Instead of running through the entire presentation I said, "Given the limited time we have, I'd like to focus on the last three slides." Rather gracefully, I was able to change gears and focus on the presentation's most important content.

After about forty-five minutes, much longer than our allotted time, someone said, "It looks like we ran a little over. Maybe we should schedule some additional time to discuss this further." When people are engaged, they often lose a sense of time and this team was very interested in what we had to say.

I replied, "Thanks so much for your time and here are a few copies of the presentation if you'd like to look them over." I was invited back to see the company multiple times and ultimately closed a deal worth well over a million dollars. To this day, my colleague and I talk about that initial meeting because, despite apparent obstacles, it went flawlessly. Don't think repetition is important? It's essential. In fact, it's truly one of the most important things you can do to improve your presentations.

Free resources at http://www.publicspeakingsimple.com/

My mentor explained it to me this way. He said that preparation and specifically repetition (repeating your presentation again and again) is like learning to drive. At first you're all knees and elbows. It takes some time to get comfortable in the car. There are just too many factors to manage. This is even more pronounced if you're learning to drive a stick shift. In addition to looking in front of you, checking the mirrors, monitoring your speed and distance between you and the car in front of you, putting your foot on the clutch and/or brake, shifting, and signaling, you have to actually steer. However, after adequate time on the road, driving becomes second nature. You're much better prepared to handle anything that comes your way. This might involve someone suddenly stopping in front of you or an obstacle in the road that requires you to shift gears. But you can only reach this level of skill through repetition, being in the car and driving a lot. The same is true with presenting. Do it over and over and over again and you'll not only get comfortable speaking, you'll start to address many other things you hadn't noticed and be prepared for every eventuality.

Free resources at http://www.publicspeakingsimple.com/

Chapter 3

Strategies for a Winning Presentation

It used to be that giving a speech was about presenting in front of a group of people, usually behind a podium and talking into a microphone. As long as you had some good information to share, people listened. But things have changed. Thanks to the Internet, smartphones, and dozens of digital devices, people's attention spans aren't what they used to be. In fact, giving a speech is seldom about information alone but rather providing some form of entertainment to your listeners. This is an important distinction and something that top speakers use to enhance presentation quality and improve message delivery.

I learned this valuable lesson my senior year of college and it has stuck with me ever since. When I attended Rutgers College School of Business in the mid-90s, a large portion of our final grade was based on a group presentation. We worked with our teams throughout the semester to prepare for this very important event. When the big day arrived, three teams were set to present, sharing their research and findings. The team with the best presentation would get an A, the second best a B, and the third would receive a C as long as certain criteria were met. Each group had a different approach to the same assignment, making for three very distinct presentations.

Group one was research focused. They developed their own surveys (primary research) and stood out in front of the student center for days polling students. They had gathered a large number of surveys and spent weeks compiling the data and crunching the numbers. In addition, they spent countless hours in the school library poring over secondary research, finding a number of references to support their position. During their presentation, they crossed every "t" and dotted every "i". And you know what? It was the most boring presentation I have ever heard.

I was part of the second team. We had done some research, just enough to validate our hypothesis. Once we had a firm direction, we put some time into our presentation to make it

Free resources at http://www.publicspeakingsimple.com/

appealing and cover most of the requirements we were asked to meet. I would say it was a fifty-fifty blend of research and presentation, addressing all of the necessary points required for a good grade. Said another way, we were able to put together a nice presentation that wasn't too much flash and not too much data.

The third team took a different approach. Made up of mostly advertising majors, I knew this team wasn't likely to offer anything of substance. At the same time, I knew their presentation was going to be good. And I wasn't disappointed. The presentation was fantastic. They filmed a video, used incredible graphics in their presentation, and told an amazing story. Oddly enough I don't think they did any research, met many of the requirements associated with the final project, or even stopped to solicit feedback. Nonetheless, they walked away with the "A."

"How can that be?" I thought to myself. I mean, we did everything we were supposed to do and our presentation was good. We followed the rules. "*Shouldn't we be rewarded*?" I thought. But soon thereafter, I realized this was a teachable moment. Life is not always about coloring within the lines. Sometimes you have to do something different, be exciting, and reach outside your boundaries. Powerful presenters do this on a regular basis to engage their audience and improve their skills. The good news is that you don't have to be Winston Churchill to engage your audience. There are a variety of techniques you can use to elevate your presentations in a meaningful way, regardless of your style. In the next section we are going to explore some valuable techniques you can use to become an effective presenter. Once you've started down the path to overcoming your fear of public speaking and feeling more confident in front of an audience you can try additional techniques to round out your presentation skills and engage your audience. Let's start with the basics for a good, meaningful presentation.

Free resources at http://www.publicspeakingsimple.com/

Beyond basic preparation

The more you put into preparing your presentation, the more you'll get out of it. This is a universal truth. We know that repletion is a key aspect of getting comfortable in front of your audience but preparation takes it one step further. The people who are the best public speakers do a lot to prepare long before they set foot on the stage. When I share this with individuals or people I train on effective public speaking, they inevitably point to someone they've come in contact with who "never prepares for anything" or seems to speak effectively without preparation. What you don't see or haven't considered it that most preparation takes place in private and doesn't always take the same form.

Take for example the salesman who is asked to stand up in the middle of a large meeting to introduce his product or service. He may not have prepared specifically for that moment, but for days, weeks, months, and maybe even years, he's been selling his product. This has prepared him more than adequately. for that on-the-spot presentation. Ask him to explain a complex topic like quantum mechanics to the room of onlookers and he would likely feel discomfort, get embarrassed, and turn into a bumbling idiot. If someone is good on their feet, they've gained confidence through dozens or even hundreds of presentations they've delivered over time.

This is why the concept of preparation is so essential. Using the techniques from earlier in this book (the rule of four, mirror, mirror, etc.) not only prepares you for the specific presentation you are about to give but also the other questions that might take you by surprise. When you see speakers easily and effortlessly present, they have put in significant preparation in one form or another. Just because you haven't seen them prepare doesn't mean they've neglected to do so.

Free resources at http://www.publicspeakingsimple.com/

When I started out in business development, I worked for an articulate speaker who always started our meetings with an introduction. After hearing him present the same introduction over and over again, I soon began to recite the same information effortlessly when called upon. Each time I delivered the introduction on my own, I became more confident and more effective. Preparation is a combination of listening, practicing, critiquing, and refining what you're saying and how you're saying it.

A quick side note. If you ever find yourself in a situation where you are called upon to speak but haven't had the opportunity to prepare, decide if you can move forward based on your prior preparation and experience. If your nerves and discomfort are too great, consider offering an alternative. When I've been in situations where I wasn't prepared, I didn't hesitate to say so. Consider using any of the following statements when you are not adequately prepared to speak:

- "Thanks, but I really don't feel prepared to talk about [*fill in the blank*] right now."

- "Would it be all right if I talk about [*fill in the blank*] at our next meeting? I don't have all the information with me."

- "Normally I wouldn't mind talking about [*fill in the blank*], but I don't feel like I'm the best person to talk about it. Perhaps [*name*] would be better for describing [*fill in the blank*]."

- "I don't feel adequately prepared to discuss [fill in the blank] but can share information about [fill in the blank]."

In my opinion you should never find yourself in a defensive position. If you're not prepared to talk about something with authority, say so. People get into trouble attempting to take impossible situations and topics head on. Admitting that you are not prepared is a lot less anxiety-provoking then being

Free resources at http://www.publicspeakingsimple.com/

asked a direct question that you can't answer with confidence. As part of your preparation, practice some of these statements or variations of them. Rehearse in your mind or role-play deferring to someone else or providing information later.

Preparation also includes readying the presentation itself, including both spoken and visual materials. Regarding the latter, I've seen everything from elaborate stage shows to black-and-white PowerPoint slides. Both grandeur and simplicity have their merits, but neither is effective unless they tell a story. It is during your preparation that you want to get comfortable with delivering the story you created, which should have a clear beginning, middle, and end. Fill in the gaps using real-world examples, data, facts, and quotes that are meaningful to your audience.

Preparation should include multiple practice runs before you stand up in front of a live audience. Do a full run-through including power point slides and any other materials or prompts you'll be using. The goal is to simulate the actual presentation environment and account for as many of the factors you'll encounter as you can. In addition to your speech, consider other requirements of your presentation:

- laptop
- tablet
- projector/screen
- audio cords
- microphone
- handouts
- lighting

Free resources at http://www.publicspeakingsimple.com/

- photography and/or video

- Q&A

By working through all of these issues as you prepare, you're virtually guaranteeing yourself a flawless presentation. Don't wait until the last minute. Get all of your ducks in a row with plenty of time to spare and you'll be rewarded with the sound of applause.

Know your material

Public speaking experts can share strategies for effective presentations and overcoming anxiety, but they can't do is provide you with subject matter expertise. If you're asked to present something you know nothing about or choose a topic you are unsure of, delivering an effective presentation will be a challenge. This may seem obvious but it happens. Whether you're asked to speak about a topic that is truly unfamiliar to you or one that you know from a limited perspective, you will likely need to bridge the gap between where you are and where you want to be, additional study or research may be required.

Being in marketing, I've been asked on many occasions to speak about a topic that I was somewhat familiar with but not a true expert. In those situations I simply picked a niche, an area I was most comfortable with, and used it to dominate my presentation. Often when asked to present, we either say yes a little too quickly or fail to define the limitations or boundaries of the presentation. I'm encouraging you to do both, let the person requesting the presentation know what you're qualified to talk about and to define your boundaries—what you are *not* willing to talk about. Once you have a clear understanding of the expectations, your preparation will be much more productive. With a focused end goal in mind, develop an outline that's comprised of what you know and the areas you'll be discussing

Free resources at http://www.publicspeakingsimple.com/

when you speak. The next step is to add some meat to your presentation, providing timely, relevant information.

It's always a good idea to review your facts, stay current with the help of industry-specific news sites (if applicable), and brush up on the latest research prior to presenting. Give yourself time to adequately research and prepare your information. One of the best ways to support your material is through the use of references and citations. That way, if there are critics sitting in the audience who disagree with your information or point of view, you can refer to the source of your information. This helps defer ownership and criticism when challenged. For example, "According to a recent Google study, 67 percent of small businesses do not generate leads through their website (Source: Google Trends)." If a small business owner says, "You're wrong, I get tons of leads through my website," you can say, "That information was according to research conducted by Google. What source are you quoting?" or "Well, you must be in the 33 percent." My point is that by knowing your material and having references from others that support your main points, vulnerability is minimized. Bringing in supporting references also adds credibility to you and your material.

If you're preparing to speak on a subject that you know little about or haven't been closely involved with recently, don't hesitate to ask the opinion of your colleagues or friends. Peer review is a technique that helps verify the accuracy of what you're presenting. By sharing openly with others you trust, you can substantiate key points and see what questions arise. This allows you to better prepare for your presentation as well as any questions that might surface from attendees.

When seeking additional information or references for my presentations, I like to use [Slideshare.net](). This is a fabulous resource and one that's significantly underutilized. Slideshare offers users the ability to upload and share, publicly or privately, digital content, such as PowerPoint presentations,

Free resources at http://www.publicspeakingsimple.com/

Word documents, and Adobe PDF Portfolios. This is great news for you because there are likely a number of presentations that others have shared that already cover your topic. It's easy to browse and view these presentations to find references or gain ideas that can enrich your own presentation. A word of caution: don't plagiarize or swipe someone else's presentation! Not only is it wrong to do, but taking someone else's work often has a negative impact on your own presentation. If you're going to present something, you must fully understand the information and have ownership of the content. If you are going to use someone's slide, please get their permission and provide full attribution.

When I use Slideshare as a resource, my goal is often to find that missing piece—the source of a chart that can justify my position or data to help me make an important point. I also use the site to do research long before I start writing my own presentation. If you visit Slideshare after your presentation is pretty much done and start poking around, I guarantee that you'll have the urge to start replacing slides in your presentation and make drastic changes. This is only going to set you back and generate last minute anxiety you don't need. Use presentations from others not to dictate your style or structure but to learn more about your topic and improve your own understanding of the material. Learning from other's presentations can strengthen your knowledge and provide some of the basic references your presentation might need to support your position.

One additional thing to consider under the topic of knowing your material is to also know your audience (which we'll look at more closely soon). If you're presenting to PhDs, for example, then it's vitally important to elevate your subject matter expertise parallel to their comprehension. Your audience will only pay attention if you are seen as a credible resource, as someone speaking at or slightly above their level. Having the right level of subject matter expertise is a great start.

Free resources at http://www.publicspeakingsimple.com/

Know your audience

Attending a presentation can be either voluntary, you decided to go on your own, or involuntary, where attendance was mandatory. Regardless of why you attend any presentation I'm sure you want to be engaged and receive something useful from the speaker. Unfortunately, many presentations are designed with a cookie cutter approach and don't take the audience into consideration regarding either the appropriate level of material or customization. I'm sure it's not uncommon for you to walk into a presentation only to start tuning out after the first five or ten minutes because the information is either not relevant or not at your level. Personally, I can't stand these presentations because if speakers aren't going to take the time to create value for me, I'm not going to give them my time or attention.

A good example would be someone speaking to newspaper publishers. If the speaker is talking about technology and says something that was obviously offensive like, "No one reads the newspaper anymore," he will lose his entire audience in an instant. If on the other hand he were to say, "I know that technology has forced many of you to move from print to digital media to gain access to an audience reading news on their smartphones, iPads, etcetera," then he would not only keep the audience engaged but would build credibility. In addition to core content, any examples, charts, graphs, and other media being presented should be related to your audience. Your audience is interested in what happens to them, in their own world, not someone else's. Remember WIIFM (what's in it for me) as an underlying theme. If you take the time to know your audience and customize your presentation to be relevant to their business, industry, or situation, you'll gain respect and create engagement.

Before you prepare a presentation, think of the audience and ask yourself, "What's unique about this audience?" and "Why should they listen to me?" When you ask and answer these

Free resources at http://www.publicspeakingsimple.com/

questions, consider not only the value of what you have to offer but also the needs they have. After identifying their needs, list three ways that you can help them. What information can you provide? What data would they find of value? Are there websites or other resources they can use to achieve their goals?

By understanding the background of your audience—who they are, their current knowledge of your topic, why they are attending the presentation—you can determine how best to design your presentation. Some time ago I was asked to do a presentation where company attendees were forced to attend. Not an ideal situation for anyone, but I took the time to do my homework and prepare accordingly. During my introduction I simply said, "I know that you didn't have a choice in attending this so session but if you give me your full attention I'll show you how to gain an extra hour each day in your work or personal life with just one three-minute activity."

The fact of the matter is that the group was not interested in another executive giving them a "rah-rah" speech about doing more for the business. Rather, they wanted to know how to improve their own lifestyle (WIIFM), which could translate into more time with their family and more time to exercise or focus on a hobby. I then proceeded to cover the necessary material but most importantly delivered on my promise. I showed them how creating a list of the top 6 things they wanted to accomplish that day, for work or pleasure, and ranking them in order of importance, could dramatically improve their productivity. After the presentation I had a long line of people who wanted to thank me for addressing their specific needs and asked me additional questions related to the topic at hand. Truthfully I was not an industry expert but I took the time to understand my audience, do some research online, and provide them what they wanted. The time I spent was greatly appreciated and helped me to engage my audience.

Free resources at http://www.publicspeakingsimple.com/

What happens if you don't know your audience? The simple answer is *Ask*. When I don't know my audience, whether giving a speech, webinar, or impromptu discussion, I always ask questions to learn more about those I'm presenting to. In fact, I refuse to give a presentation until I know my audience and how I can create value for them. This can be done in a variety of ways and simply requires asking a few simple questions. One technique is to say, "By a show of hands, how many people here [fill in the blank]?" The great thing about this technique is that everyone in the room participates in some manner, giving you a clear understanding of audience composition. Alternatively you can ask the audience some questions about their background or experience as a whole. Inevitably someone will serve as the spokesperson and provide more information about the group. With the help of polling and chat features, getting feedback on webinars is also very easy.

This step is essential for success and I can't stress it enough. Without a complete profile of your audience, you're like a ship without a rudder—you'll end up on the rocks. Take the time to understand your audience and what information they want to hear. When you have a clear direction your presentation will flow more readily and the audience is more likely to be interested in what you have to say.

Overcome your habits

Now that you've laid the groundwork and have started down the path of getting ready for your presentation, it's time to address the symptoms of your anxiety head-on. In addition to utilizing methods that reduce feelings of anxiety (relabeling, mental rehearsal, etc.), it's also important to face your most challenging habits. I label behaviors like saying "Umm" between every sentence, dry mouth, and shakiness, as habits. Many of my students ask why I refer to these as "habits" when they are not something you control. The answer is simple, they

Free resources at http://www.publicspeakingsimple.com/

are in your control – you're just experiencing them automatically which is also known as a habit. And all habits can be broken!

I've had issues with each of the before mentioned habits and broke each one of them. Here's what you can do to remove these nagging habits and establish new, empowering habits that enhance your presentations.

<u>Saying "Umm"</u> – Have you ever noticed when presenting you tend to repeat undesirable phrases? *"It may sound something, umm, like this. Umm, the next thing I want to discuss, umm, is umm, something about the weather."* Or perhaps, *"Like um someone who wants to like talk about a topic but like doesn't have a clear grasp of like, what they want to discuss".* Yeah, things can be this bad but there's an easy way to break this habit – whatever your undesirable catchphrase may be.

My mentor shared this habit busting technique with me a long time ago and it's incredibly effective. Repeat the catch phrase out loud over and over again: "Umm, Umm, Umm, Umm, Umm, Umm, Umm, Umm.." Try doing this for a few minutes multiple times each day, whenever you can. In a short while you'll notice yourself becoming more aware of the habit and correcting yourself or eliminating the word even before it's spoken. The reason this technique works, is because currently use the phrase subconsciously, without your knowledge. Repeating the phrase out loud makes you aware that you're using it repeatedly. Once at a conscious level, you have the leverage to change it. Give it a try and find the habit of repetition fading away and eliminated.

<u>Dry Mouth</u> – If you've ever been nervous, you probably experienced dry mouth where it feels as though you have a few cotton balls stuffed in there. For those of us who have experienced this, it's pretty close to the worst feeling you can have during a presentation, making it difficult or impossible to speak. In addition to being a habit associated with public

speaking, dry mouth can also be caused by medications, the aging process and health conditions, such as depression, stroke or diabetes.

This habit was a real issue for me and it took a lot of trial and error to find the perfect remedy. I was able to find relief by doing two simple things. The first is to ALWAYS have a water bottle with you before and during your presentation. When traveling, I'll even pack a couple of water bottles in my suitcase and write my name on them with a Sharpie. Don't expect your host to have water for you. By sipping your water during your presentation, you can alleviate your dry mouth to some degree. When applying the second step, proper breathing, you can dramatically reduce the symptoms associated with dry mouth. Practice your inhaling through your nose on a regular basis. As you build a habit of better breathing, your dry mouth is greatly diminished. When sensing dry mouth on stage, focus on breathing through your nose. This has a positive and immediate impact on your habit.

Shakiness – Physical habits that show anxiety are prevalent among public speakers. Whether your hands seem to shake uncontrollably or you can't stop your foot from tapping, these habits can undermine confidence. The best way to break this type of habit is with a two-step process. The first is minimization. Essentially the goal is to minimize your exposure to the audience. For example, if you tap your foot or shake, standing behind a podium can shield you from onlookers. Another helpful technique is to reduce the use of visuals you interact with on a physical level. For example, don't hold up any papers or items for display. Instead, integrate them directly into your PowerPoint presentation. If you start shaking while holding something up, everyone's going to see it and it will make you feel self-conscious.

The second step is to apply the same technique we discussed during the first habit (repetition) we discussed with slight variation. Begin by shaking your hands while holding an item, if

Free resources at http://www.publicspeakingsimple.com/

this is the habit you wish to break, then pause and take two deep breaths through your nose while relaxing. Practicing this multiple times create a new habit that is formed once the old habit begins to occur. Even though you are not in the same environment, replicating the physical symptoms will trigger many of the same brain cells associated with the habit when occurring in front of a live audience. Through repetition – practicing multiple times over a short period will create a new, empowering pattern that occurs whenever the habit begins, starting at the sub-conscious level.

Lay the groundwork

One of the most effective strategies for making an impact is clarity and repetition. If you want people to listen and take away something of value, you must first lay the groundwork. I like to call this "setting the table." Before you can focus on serving a special meal, you must first set the table appropriately. Plates, cups, napkins, maybe even some candlelight. Without adequate preparation, your meal would be dull and uninviting. To engage your audience from the start and keep their attention, you must set expectations. Setting the table means that you tell your audience what you're going to talk about, talk about it, and then summarize appropriately. The key is getting the first step right, letting them know what to expect and then delivering on your promise. I know this concept is very simple and straightforward, but you'd be amazed at how many people jump right into their presentations without a clear roadmap or any expectations of what will be covered. If you fail to set the table, your audience may get lost or have false expectations.

When you're presenting always remember that you're the leader and others need a clear agenda to follow. Not having a clear path toward your desired outcome presents a number of risks and problems you want to avoid. I've seen many speakers neglect the important step of defining outcomes and articulating a clear agenda. Because of this oversight, they lost control of

Free resources at http://www.publicspeakingsimple.com/

their audience or failed to deliver an effective message. You can avoid these pitfalls by laying the groundwork with a simple and clear agenda that meets the needs of your audience.

Personally, I like to lay the groundwork immediately with a simple statement as part of the introduction. Your statement should be something like, "Today I'm going to start with a personal story, talk to you about [fill in the blank], and share my findings on [fill in the blank]. We'll review all of the key points and finish with questions and answers." Keep in mind that you don't need to present a long and complex agenda. The goal is to keep things simple. By laying the groundwork you put yourself in control and manage audience expectations. If members of your audience had misconceptions about what you were covering, they won't be disappointed after you've presented for forty minutes or more without touching on their issues.

I equate this strategy to an effective teamwork exercise. If you were given a specific task that was simultaneously communicated to you and your team, you would have a good chance of working together toward your desired outcome. On the other hand, if nothing was communicated, or if only a few people had a true idea of what needed to be accomplished, it's unlikely that your team would be as successful. Keep this in mind before your next presentation. Jumping in and starting your presentation without a clear roadmap can lead to quickly getting off course. The best speakers take the time to set expectations and determine a destination. Some speakers use stories to set the table; others provide an outline or statement. Use what you're most comfortable with but don't skip this important step.

Start an outline

This may sound "old school," but once you have a good understanding of your audience and their needs, the best place to start preparing for your presentation is with an outline. The more effort you put into knowing your audience and creating a framework for your presentation, the easier it becomes to develop. It may seem silly, but I've spent hours developing presentation outlines to make sure I'm framing my presentation properly—making it engaging, informative, and goal-oriented. Outlines may be simple but aren't necessarily easy to produce. Creating an effective outline follows the 80/20 rule (aka Pareto's principle). By focusing on the right 20 percent, you're doing 80 percent of the work. Good outlines not only position you for success but also make the creation of a worthwhile presentation much easier.

As you sit down to write your outline, think in terms of a mind map. A mind map is a way of organizing your thoughts and ideas using a clean sheet of paper. Essentially, you start with a single idea in the middle and think through all of the related ideas or topics. The goal of [mind mapping](#) is to brainstorm all of the ideas you want to address and communicate to your audience. It's likely that you won't include all of them in your actual presentation but it can certainly help to identify key message points and takeaways for your audience. Give yourself permission to brainstorm and put all of your ideas, potential topics, illustrations, and stories on paper. Once you collect all of your ideas in a single location, start to organize them in a logical manner. Group similar ideas, throw away anything that's irrelevant based on your understanding of the audience, and narrow down the specific areas to include in your outline. After taking this step you're ready to develop a winning presentation.

Free resources at http://www.publicspeakingsimple.com/

Chapter 4

Creating Your Winning Presentation

Free resources at http://www.publicspeakingsimple.com/

As you brainstorm different aspects of your presentation and identify themes, translate them into a loose outline. The method that I've used for years begins with a basic mind map as noted earlier. After identifying different themes or key points I want to discuss, I write them down on index cards or sticky notes. I'll even include sticky notes that refer to stories or examples because they are such a critical aspect of my presentations. I then take the sticky notes and organize them on a white board or wall, moving things around until the information begins to flow. Once that's complete, I'm ready to develop an outline.

The outline should include an introduction, laying the groundwork for your presentation, key ideas, stories or examples, and a conclusion. Read through your outline again and again until you've fully fleshed out your ideas and created a solid template for your presentation. After going through this exercise, put your outline down and give yourself a day before revisiting. Some people like to move directly from their outline to creating a PowerPoint presentation. Others prefer to write out what they are going to say word for word. You have to find the method that works best for you. I recommend against writing out or reading every word of your presentation. This usually results in staring at your papers the whole time as opposed to making eye contact with the audience. Furthermore, if something throws you off and cause you to vary only slightly from your written word, you could become disoriented or confused.

By developing a solid outline, one that you're truly comfortable with, you can dramatically enhance the quality of your presentation while making you much more comfortable in front of your audience.

The introduction

Speakers set the tone from the word "go." One could argue that the overall tone of a presentation starts long before a speaker utters his first syllable. With the advent of modern technology the art of beginning a presentation with new and creative tactics, from music to pyrotechnics, is not out of the question. As I noted earlier in the book effective presentations are part flash and part substance. You need to think through your introduction very carefully based on the audience size, makeup, and setting to start off on the right foot.

An important distinction to keep in mind is that an introduction doesn't always have to be about you. Each introduction needs to be customized based on your personal preferences and the audience you're speaking to. Many speakers start their presentations by asking questions, addressing a common concern, defining the agenda, or telling a story. In fact their intro may change each and every time they present. It's essential that you remain flexible in your approach, doing what's best for you and your audience.

I'm not trying to make the art of introductions confusing or difficult to grasp but rather explain that there's no "right" answer—it all depends on you and your audience. I recently attended a conference where the majority of the speakers started off with questions for the audience about their area of expertise. After hearing the responses, they laid the groundwork and then finally introduced themselves. And it worked very well. Would it have been as effective with a different audience? I don't know. Your goal should be to try a few different formats and see which ones you are most comfortable with. For example, you may prefer to always start your presentations with a story followed by your bio. Alternatively, you might like the person introducing you to give a lengthy bio so you don't have to. Find the style you're most comfortable with and stick with it.

A good rule of thumb for introductions is to never leave out your credentials altogether. Try to provide some background within the first third of your presentation. This is important for setting the tone and giving the audience a reason to listen you. Let's

Free resources at http://www.publicspeakingsimple.com/

take a look at a few different types of introductions to help you think through a format that will work for your style and audience.

Introductions can be done using a variety of formats based on the room type, size of audience, and technological capabilities. One of my favorite introductions was at a corporate meeting where co-presenters entered from the back of a very large room after their bios were read by a company executive. As the presenters walked in, upbeat music played, and they threw out T-shirts and other promotional items to the audience. You could feel the excitement. Not only did this put everyone in a great frame of mind, it also helped to put the speakers at ease. Now you might be saying to yourself, "That's not me. I can't run into a room with music playing and start handing out T-shirts!" That's OK because the goal is to realize that introductions don't have to be boring. You're going to see a lot of introductions as you observe other speakers, and they're all done differently. Take notes on what you like, what suits your style, and what you'd like to replicate for your own presentations. This is how you learn and develop your own personal style.

On a separate occasion, I found myself in a large ballroom with nearly a thousand people in attendance. I knew that everyone in the room was related to the publishing industry so after I was introduced by the MC, I asked everyone to stand up. Then, I proceeded to ask questions of increasing criteria (e.g., "Sit down if you've never read the news online. Sit down if you spend less than five hours a week reading the news…").

The whole point was to create an introduction that would position my speech appropriately. I went on to talk about the growing number of people consuming information online and how consumption of digital media is based on a variety of factors. It wasn't until I was a few slides in that I spoke about my experience and credentials.

Free resources at http://www.publicspeakingsimple.com/

You should always try a variety of introductions because what looks like a good fit may not work for every audience. When considering different types of introductions, ask yourself some questions of your own: Who's my audience? Why are they listening to me? What's the goal? Also consider logistical questions that may limit what you can or can't do. Am I going to stand in front of the audience on the floor? Would I rather stand behind the podium? Use slides? Be introduced? Give some thought to your preferred method of introduction. Find something that fits your personality and style. The introduction sets the tone and should be treated as an opportunity to start on the right foot.

A quick side note to consider: I for one like to be introduced before giving a presentation. Having someone who is associated with the audience provide an introduction always seems to ease the tension and add credibility to the speaker. That being said, introductions shouldn't be left to chance. If you're in a position where someone is going to provide an introduction for you, give them bullet points or a bio they can read. It takes only a few minutes to develop and can be customized for the audience you're addressing. Remember that your introduction can take a variety of forms and the best introductions create excitement and enthusiasm for you and your presentation.

What if there isn't anyone to introduce you? The answer is simple, introduce yourself. Never assume that people know who you are or what you do. I can't tell you how many times I've been in large meetings or presentations where people just got up and started talking. I'm sure many people in the room thought, "Who are you and why should I listen to you?" As you make your introduction remember to position yourself appropriately for the audience you're speaking to. For example, if I were speaking to fellow authors I might say, "Hello, my name is Mike Fleischner, and I'm the author of *Public Speaking Made Simple* and a number of other self-improvement books." On the other hand, if I were speaking to a group of entrepreneurs I might start by saying, "Hello, my name

Free resources at http://www.publicspeakingsimple.com/

is Mike Fleischner, founder of the Made Simple Media Company. I've been publishing books for a number of years across multiple disciplines, including marketing, self-help, and personal development."

It's likely that entrepreneurs would be less interested in an author and be more inclined to listen to a successful business owner. Always remember to customize your introduction to be genuine, honest, and of high interest to your audience. As an alternative, you can forego the bio and first address a specific need. This form of introduction is also very common and usually resonates with your audience. For example, "I'm really excited to be here today to talk about recycling. Did you know that the average American uses six hundred fifty pounds of paper each year? By a show of hands, how many people here recycle? During this presentation I'm going to share..." After you connect with your audience and get through your introduction, be sure to position yourself as an expert and provide the necessary background or bio.

Remember, the best time to make a lasting impression on your audience is at the start of your presentation. One way to do this is by telling a story or showing a video. As Internet access is more readily available, regardless of the presentation location, using visuals to tell a story is becoming more common. Stories engage audiences and generate interest like nothing else can. Using multimedia, especially video, can communicate a strong message quickly and jump-start your presentation even before you say a word. This puts your audience in the right frame of mind and can prepare them for what's to come. The great thing about video is that, thanks to YouTube and other video-sharing sites, there's plenty to choose from. You can find the video that illustrates your point or puts your audience in the right frame of mind. If you're comfortable sharing a story without the help of video, then go for it. The point is that introductions can be fun and don't always have to follow the same pattern. I recommend searching the web for meaningful stories or videos to share. Using real stories, even if they don't come from personal experiences, can have a positive impact on your audience and

Free resources at http://www.publicspeakingsimple.com/

make for a strong introduction. A word of caution: using multimedia is great but you must be sure that you have the necessary equipment to deliver audio and visual. Don't rely on multimedia without testing your equipment. I've learned the hard way that not every podium is set up with audio and/or video hookups. Even if the hookups are present, they may not work for the computer you're using. For this reason I only use video introductions if I've had the opportunity to test the actual equipment I'll be using or do a dry run in the room where I'll be presenting.

Once you've mastered your introduction and you are satisfied the audience will have a general sense of what you're talking about, it's time to organize the rest of your speech in a way that will leave a lasting impression.

The core presentation

There's a lot that goes into delivering an effective presentation. In fact, I've spent days writing and rewriting slides to get everything just perfect —but it doesn't have to work that way. My goal in this section is to share some simple techniques that work time and again for organizing your content and delivering presentations that meet or exceed expectations.

The best place to start is with the most basic structure, called the linear format. This is ideal for anyone starting out or even those with advanced skills who want to keep things simple as they prepare for speeches. Presenting in a linear format means that you move from introduction to conclusion in as few steps as possible. Many speakers, including myself, generally move from point A to point B one step at a time. We may tell some stories along the way or take a couple of detours, but moving in a linear progression is the easiest and often the most effective way to deliver a strong presentation.

Free resources at http://www.publicspeakingsimple.com/

The linear approach is the method I use most often and consider it the bread and butter of good presenters. The alternative is to take a nonlinear approach, where you focus on key ideas—delivering them in isolation—and then bring everything together at the end of your presentation. A mentor of mine introduced me to this model and expanded my paradigm to consider different presentation styles. He described the method as akin to crossing a river. Due to the water's temperature, current, and obstacles, speakers carefully lay stones in order to cross to the other side. Using this analogy, the goal is the same, to traverse the river. However, the method you use to get there is rarely linear. You may go a few steps forward, jump off to a stone on one side, and then move in different directions until you hit all of the high points. This makes the journey much more interesting and provides room for creativity. However, doing this successfully takes some skill and a good deal of experience. I recommend reserving this technique until you are more advanced because it takes a good deal of practice to pull off successfully but it makes for a very engaging presentation. This is especially true if you tend to get distracted easily by shiny objects. Most people are very comfortable walking a straight line but have reservations about jumping from stone to stone as they cross rivers. If you're just starting your speaking journey, begin with the linear approach and then evolve toward finding various ways to cross rivers gracefully.

The linear approach. This is all about moving through multiple stages, one by one, to reach a desired end. As we discussed earlier, you lay the groundwork by telling your audience who you are and what you'll be sharing with them. It's also helpful to explain what order you'll be presenting your information in. This helps to set expectations and keep you in complete control. A good example of a linear introduction that keeps things organized would look like this:

"Hello everyone, my name is Michael Fleischner. I'm a marketing expert who has been selling and marketing products

Free resources at http://www.publicspeakingsimple.com/

over the last ten years. Today I'm going to talk to you about pricing theory. First I'm going to explain what pricing theory is, then I'll share a number of different examples of products and pricing models. We'll explore each pricing model one by one and then summarize by highlighting the different pricing models you can use for your own business. Then we'll have about ten minutes for Q&A."

That's it. Laying out a linear presentation doesn't have to be difficult. In this example we simply introduced ourselves and laid out a very simple agenda. When you clearly define the scope of your presentation, it's much more likely to stay on course. Here's another example:

"Hi there, my name is Michael Fleischner, and I'm the author of a number of how-to books. My goal today is to share my personal story with you of how I started writing, turned my content into print and digital books, and sold them on Amazon.com. By the end of today's presentation, you'll have specific, tangible steps you can take for publishing your books or other written works as well."

The above approach is linear—you're following a straight line to a defined outcome, articulating what comes first, second, third, and so on. The best way to identify the appropriate steps for your presentation begins with a clear understanding of the presentation goal. Get a clear picture of what you want the audience to take away: What should they learn from your presentation? Once you identify the goal, define the steps for getting there one at a time. And keep it simple! You should have five steps or fewer that lead to your desired outcome. This is essential to keep your presentations clear and concise.

As an example, let me introduce you to a fictitious character named Tom. He's an engineer who has been asked to present the company's capabilities for improving work processes. The goal of the presentation is to develop a compelling case as to why this company should hire his engineering firm to improve

Free resources at http://www.publicspeakingsimple.com/

business processes and help reduce operational costs. You might be saying to yourself, *"boring"* or perhaps, "That sounds like something that I might have to do." I'm sure we can all relate on some level. The point here is that Tom is going to structure his presentation using a linear approach. Here is some insight into his thought process.

"OK," Tom thinks to himself. "The goal here is to showcase how we can improve business processes for the company and help to reduce their costs. We've done this before for other companies and have shown some pretty good results," he thinks to himself. "I suppose we need to introduce ourselves first and then start building a case based on what I know about the company. Although it's not much, I do have some ideas about their market and how our services might be a good fit." Tom has started to think through, in a linear fashion, how to organize his presentation. Over the next thirty minutes or so he drafts an outline that lays out the steps he will follow. After some brainstorming and a few revisions, he comes up with the following:

I.   Introduction

        a. People in attendance

        b. Company history

II. Problem Statement

        a. Overview of possible challenges (ask/confirm)

        b. Explore other challenges we see others experiencing

        c. What happens when issues are not addressed properly

Free resources at http://www.publicspeakingsimple.com/

III. Company Capabilities

    a. Our strengths

    b. Our limitations—issues we don't address

IV. Proof of Concept

    a. Other clients we've helped

    b. Methods we've used to improve outcomes

    c. Measurable results

    d. What others say about us (social proof)

V. Conclusion

    a. Questions & Next Steps

Using this fictitious example, you can see the linear approach at work. Personally I know nothing about engineering but realize that doing what you can to understand the needs of your prospects and customers is essential. One could argue that the first part of the presentation should include some probing questions for your prospect so you know what specific areas need to be addressed. I firmly recommend this approach immediately following introductions or your business summary whenever you do not have as much information as you desire.

It's always a good idea to get clarity on why you're there, presenting. This means assessing the situation with others in the room. The saying, "seek first to understand than be understood" comes to mind. In essence you are clarifying goals and expectations. Once you understand the purpose, you can

Free resources at http://www.publicspeakingsimple.com/

move toward showcasing your capabilities and providing possible remedies. At the end of your presentation, you'll conclude and discuss the next steps your audience should take. The above is only an example but the purpose is to lay out a number of basic steps that build on one another, taking you toward a specific goal. Embellishing the outline with personal stories is also a great way to enhance the value of your presentation.

Developing presentations for small or large audiences should follow the linear approach outlined above, beginning with an introduction and including specific steps necessary to reach your conclusion. Think in terms of step 1, step 2, step 3 until you reach your final destination. Refine your steps again and again until you've made your outline as simple as possible.

Not too long ago, I did a webinar on search engine optimization, another passion of mine. Using the linear approach, I was able to create an outline that was both basic and effective. When all was said and done, my outline looked something like this:

I. Introduction

II. Search engine optimization (SEO) basics

    a. Why search engines are important

    b. The most important factors that determine rankings

    c. Recent changes to search engine algorithms

III. How to optimize your own website

    a. On page optimization best practices

Free resources at http://www.publicspeakingsimple.com/

        b.   Off page optimization best practices

IV.   Measuring results

        a.   Importance of tracking

        b.   Tools you can use to monitor results

V.   Conclusion

Search engine optimization is a very complex subject, but if you can't simplify your content, how do you expect others to truly understand what you're sharing? To be fair, the final presentation integrated a number of graphs, examples, and stories, but it was all developed using a simple linear outline.

When you're developing presentations using a linear approach give yourself some time to get comfortable with the process of direct progression. Even though I would consider this simple, it's not always easy. Taking complex topics and breaking them down into logical steps takes time and practice. The good news is that it won't take long to master this approach and it serves as a very strong foundation for persuasive presentations. A guiding principal I've used over the years, especially if I'm having a hard time laying out my presentation is to ask the question, "What has to happen before [fill in the blank] can happen?" To use the example above, "What has to happen before I talk about search engine optimization?" The answer is that I have to introduce myself and explain why search engine optimization is so important. If I don't establish some level of credibility, the audience will never be engaged or want to listen to what I have to say.

The best way to get comfortable with the linear approach to writing speeches and presentations is to actually do the work. Before your next speaking engagement, take a few minutes to relax and think about the key points you want to communicate. Put pen to paper and list each of your key points in

Free resources at http://www.publicspeakingsimple.com/

progression. What comes first? Second? Third? If you're struggling to get ideas, now would be a good time to pull out the index cards or sticky notes you created while brainstorming topics. Continue to work on your outline until you have all of the necessary steps to reach your desired conclusion. Doing this over and over again makes the process easier and more effective.

The nonlinear approach. For some of you who are more advanced, getting from point A to point B doesn't need to be a straight line. If you want to make your presentation more dynamic and are ready to progress beyond the linear approach, I recommend you do so in the following stages. They provide a natural progression for enhancing your presentation and diversifying your content. Instead of jumping to something wild and crazy, begin with Stage 1 and when ready, progress to stage two.

Stage 1

The first stage is developing your presentation with a few rest stops along the way. This method is similar to the linear path but much like a road trip, you're going to pull over a few times on your journey for various reasons (taking pictures, fueling up, etc.). Keep in mind that your goal should be to minimize your side trips and keep them short and relevant. You should begin by listing the main points you want to cover and then identify some short stories, sounds bites, or references you can use to embellish your content or reinforce each main point. Not only will your audience find engaging but it provides a natural bridge back to your presentation. Try to use specific examples including names, places, dates, and so on. This makes examples more credible.

It took me a long time to get reasonably good at telling stories. Even so, I certainly don't consider myself an expert storyteller. I only use stories that reinforce a point or illustrate an idea that

Free resources at http://www.publicspeakingsimple.com/

I'm trying to communicate. This is really the first step in developing presentations that are a little less linear and slightly more creative. As always, the best thing you can do is share your stories with others to see if they resonate and are clearly articulated before sharing them in a presentation.

As you practice your presentation, rehearse your stories again and again. The more you do the more proficient and comfortable you'll be when sharing them with your audience. This is one of the key aspects and differentiators of a nonlinear presentation style. I know that by retelling stories it becomes easier to share them with various audiences and improve upon them. Think about customizing your stories based on key messages you wish to deliver and the goals of your presentation. This is essential for delivering a flawless presentation that is non-linear.

Stage 2

Once you've mastered the art of delivering a solid presentation with a few short stops along the way (to share your stories, data, etc.), it's time to traverse the river using your own path. There are a number of ways this can take shape during your presentation but the most common approach involves audience participation. I strongly recommend that you don't try this on a whim but rather wait until you've mastered the basic presentation skills and feel comfortable in front of a significant audience.

Audience participation can take place in a variety of formats; however, they all involve some type of interaction with an audience either one-on-one or a team approach that often involves presentations and a critique. What I like about audience participation is that participants are more engaged and often take away something tangible they can apply to their lives in some way—school, work, personal.

Free resources at http://www.publicspeakingsimple.com/

To involve the audience, you must have a clear goal in mind. How do you plan to use the audience to reinforce the main points you want to share? What type of interaction or activity can drive your main point home? The more involved your audience throughout the presentation, engaging in activities and ultimately teaching back the concepts you're presenting, the more powerful your presentation becomes. This advanced technique has tremendous and lasting impact but must be well planned, rehearsed, and organized.

Keep in mind there are varying degrees of audience participation. In fact, I've been involved in presentations where merely having the audience stand or raise their hands has left a significant impact on the content being presented. I remember a number of years ago, during a presentation about online shopping habits, I asked an audience of about 200 people to stand up if they had ever shopped on Amazon.com. Nearly every person in the room stood up – talk about making a point! I've also been at the opposite side of the spectrum where I had audiences divide into small work teams and present back to the larger group with their key points or findings. The type of interaction you solicit needs to be based on your presentation, goals, and whether or not involving the audience is appropriate.

One thing to keep in mind as you consider involving the audience is that you are the leader and must remain in control of the room. That means you must be the one to calmly and firmly assert yourself and the agenda you want for your audience. Don't let the loudest audience member take you off course. Also, you can't expect your audience to figure everything out on their own. Your role is to serve as a coach, guiding them through the exercise you've tasked them with. After a fixed period of time, bring things together in a very disciplined and deliberate way with a clear process for extracting the information you expect.

When I talk about audience participation and taking a nonlinear approach to public speaking, some people think that means you can't prepare. Actually the opposite is true. Relying on audience participation means you must do even more to manage your presentation and prepare for unexpected situations. Think of a magician. He may call up complete strangers from the audience to help him with a trick but is confident in terms of how things are going to turn out. This is because he has done a great deal of preparation prior to the show and provides direction throughout the interaction. You need to do the same if you wish to have things turn out successfully.

Regardless of which presentation format you use, linear or nonlinear, your success really comes down to knowing your content and having adequate preparation. One of the best ways to be effective using either presentation format is to thoroughly know your material. When you know your material and are comfortable presenting it, your audience will become much more receptive and engaged in what you have to say.

Subject matter expertise

To create a winning presentation you must have command of your subject matter. This is an absolute *must* before being able to present in a confident manner to anyone. I can't tell you how many times I've sat in presentations where people clearly had no idea of what they were talking about, and it showed. They were often nervous, spent most of their time reading word-for-word from their slides, or got tripped up by a seemingly innocuous question from the audience. Regardless of what led to their downfall, they clearly did not take learning their material seriously enough. Assume there will always be someone in the audience who knows more than you, and that's OK. The audience is not looking for a flawless presentation, but rather just enough to illustrate your grasp of the subject matter. This establishes your credibility and has a direct impact on your ability to engage audiences.

Free resources at http://www.publicspeakingsimple.com/

Some people think that being a subject matter expert requires a lifetime of study, published research, and years of practical experience. I'd argue that being a subject matter expert simply means that you're either knowledgeable about a particular subject or have lived it in some regard. Whether that means having something like on-the-job training or intimate knowledge through hands-on experience, you have a practical understanding of your subject. A good example of this is the person speaking about cancer. Let's assume for this example that the person spent the last couple of years living with a loved one who was personally affected by the disease. If they present on the challenge of living with someone who's been diagnosed with cancer, they are a subject matter expert because they've experienced it. If on the other hand they try to present as someone who has suffered from the disease but never had it themselves, their credibility is shaky at best. Subject matter experience means that you're qualified to talk about your topic. That's why the most effective presentations are those that draw from the personal experience of the presenter.

You can illustrate your subject matter expertise in a number of ways. My favorite, and the easiest way, is to share a personal story with your audience. As long as the story is related to your subject, it can establish you as an expert. Another way is sharing your credentials, work history, or experience. If any of these things are aligned with your subject matter, then you're off to a good start.

You might ask, what happens if I'm speaking about something that's slightly outside of my comfort zone? How can I establish myself as a subject matter expert or credible speaker? This is a question I receive quite often. People can be asked to speak on topics outside their areas of expertise for a variety of reasons, and it is usually one of the most anxiety-provoking situations that can arise. The remedy is in how you choose to deal with the situation to ensure a successful outcome.

Free resources at http://www.publicspeakingsimple.com/

I'll share with you some of the techniques I've personally used when asked to speak about subjects I know very little about. With effort, you can fill the role as an expert without all of the background experience that is usually required. These techniques involve clarifying your experience, sharing data, research, using support, and quoting others who are well-known in the field. By using these techniques, you are positioning yourself as the conduit to tangible resources rather than as the direct source of expertise. In fact, as you listen to some of today's top speakers, you'll notice they frequently quote the work of others to reinforce their own credibility and validate the points they're making. One of my favorite quotes when thinking about leveraging resources is from W. Edwards Deming who said, "In God we trust, all others bring data."

Let's explore your options for mitigating this situation a little further. On one occasion where I did not have subject matter expertise (speaking to a pharmaceutical team) I did the unthinkable. I quickly admitted my ignorance of pharmaceuticals and publicly announced my shortcomings. This may seem foreign to some but it's actually OK to admit when you do not have subject matter expertise, and, quite honestly, it's preferable to admit your weaknesses sooner rather than later. The technique that I used was not to simply state my shortcomings, but to also share my strengths. After admitting my ignorance in pharmaceuticals, I quickly shared my background and success in the industry they were trying to sell into. This helped to manage expectations and show how I could be relevant to the conversation. Just a few minutes into the presentation I began to share specific experiences and insights into the target market that could benefit the audience and they became excited. My experience was grounded in years of working with the target market and delivering tangible results. That's what people came to hear, despite my lack of pharmaceutical experience.

In addition to admitting my shortcomings, I made sure to quote others from the pharmaceutical industry to establish credibility. The key to effectively quoting others is to be relevant and

Free resources at http://www.publicspeakingsimple.com/

accurate. Throwing misdirected or unfounded quotes into any presentation is a recipe for disaster. Focus your efforts on finding quotes that reinforce key points you're trying to make throughout your presentation. There are a variety of websites, such as http://www.brainyquote.com and www.famousquotes.com that help you quickly and easily find quotes relevant for virtually any situation. Such additions position you as an authority when integrated properly into your presentation.

Quotes from established experts help to reinforce key concepts. I like to think of this technique as providing instant validation to any speaker. If you're finding it difficult to locate a direct quote, use quotes that reinforce a main idea. For example, "If you want to make improvements to your public speaking, keep trying. Most people give up way too soon. Did you know that Thomas Edison recorded more than ten thousand failures on how to make the incandescent light bulb before he succeeded?" Using a famous reference or quote to support a main idea helps to establish credibility.

Using data and research are also powerful tools for positioning yourself as a subject matter expert. Whenever you start a sentence with, "According to a recent study…," people lower their walls and become more open to new ideas. If there was a study, it must be true, right? Well, not really, but studies certainly lend credibility to what you're presenting.

Remember earlier I mentioned that there will likely be one person in the audience who knows more than you do? He or she is going to need a little extra in order to be persuaded to your point of view. This is why integrating research that others have done is such a valuable technique for any presenter. By referring to credible research, you place the focus on a resource or third party. That way if someone in the room questions the research, the doubt expressed has less of an impact on your credibility and becomes more of a discussion on proper research methodologies. Even so, I've been in

Free resources at http://www.publicspeakingsimple.com/

situations where I used research from a third party that people questioned. I quickly learned that having more than one source is ideal.

If you're going to quote research, provide additional information about the source. For example, 'In a ComScore survey of more than six thousand tablet owners in the US, researchers found the Kindle Fire has more female than male users, while iPad skews to males." In this example two very important pieces of information are provided: the source and the sample size. This helps to establish the validity of your research and minimize challenges from the audience. When quoting research or data, always include the source of the research (who conducted or published the survey) and sample size. It goes without saying that the larger the sample size, the more believable the data. Sometimes, instead of trying to impress "Mr. Negative," should there be one, it's better to engage him and ask for his opinion or if he can explain a topic on your agenda. This can diffuse the situation and disarm the negativity.

One of the things I really like to do with my presentations is include any references in the footer of the appropriate PowerPoint slide. By placing your citation at the bottom of a slide, individuals who access your presentation can quickly navigate to a source. This is also a great way to share additional resources that are relevant to the topic you're covering. Often times during presentations people will ask you to repeat a website URL or source. Including resource links in slide footer saves time and helps the audience easily access important information.

It's also a good idea to leverage the expertise of others when venturing into areas for which you do not have direct experience. To this end, I've even brought others with me to address questions during the Q&A section or for specific parts of my presentation. Sometimes just introducing and having a credentialed industry expert with you is enough to establish credibility (through association).

Free resources at http://www.publicspeakingsimple.com/

The most important thing you can do when asked to speak outside your area of expertise is to determine which combination of techniques works best for you. Are you going to admit that you don't have direct experience and focus on what you can provide? Use data and research to make key points? Integrate quotes that support your point of view? Or are you going to bring a subject matter expert to be at your site? Likely using them all would be too much, so it's important to do your homework and customize your approach for the audience. The more you do so, the more relaxed and effective you will be.

In this section, we talked about different ways to prepare and deliver your presentations; linear or nonlinear, as well as subject matter expertise—an important component to effective speech delivery. But delivering a winning presentation takes more than a general format and content knowledge. It also requires an understanding of how to modify your presentation based on your audience as well as effective tools for getting you message across and creating value.

Effective formats and delivery methods

There's more than one way to give a good presentation and I'd be remiss if I didn't cover the best practices for delivering presentations across different formats and media. In this section, I'll share some of the most effective techniques I've experienced for preparing and delivering presentations through different methods, including one-on-one presentations, small groups, and large groups. I'll also share best practices for using PowerPoint, Skype, and webinar platforms (such as GoToMeeting and Webex).

Not all presentations are created equal but the basics always apply. By mastering the steps we've already discussed regarding adequate planning and preparation, you are now in a position to modify your presentation based on format. With experience you will become much more comfortable moving

Free resources at http://www.publicspeakingsimple.com/

between different presentation formats and media types. I encourage you to seek out new opportunities to present in each of the following formats as often as possible.

These are the most common presentation formats but can certainly apply to new or different situations. For example, when starting my public speaking career in earnest, I found that many of the same techniques that worked in one-one-one sessions would also work for telephone interviews. Focus on your skills and your unique audience to deliver a quality presentation.

One-on-one presentations. Some people are great when presenting one on one. This may take place at a desk or table, in front of a white board, or sitting side by side with someone as they look at your computer screen. The most effective way to communicate when giving a one-on-one presentation is by using many of the techniques already described: using a linear path, offering an introduction and agenda, and having a conclusion that reiterates key points you want your (small) audience to take away. The most important aspect of giving one-on-one presentations, whether at school, work, or another setting, is to minimize distractions. You may scoff at the idea or think it's a no-brainer, but the reality is that most people do not consciously control their environment to adequately minimize distractions. For example, when someone comes to your office, do you quiet your phone and close your laptop or turn off your computer screen? Do you find a quiet place to give your presentation that is free from outside distractions? Before sitting down with someone, think about the environment you're in and what you can do to focus 100 percent of your attention on the individual you'll be sharing information with. This goes a long way in terms of how receptive your audience will be to the information you share.

If you're nervous presenting to an individual, think of the various aides you have at your disposal to minimize anxiety. Although I strongly recommend making direct eye contact, some individuals find this to be nerve-racking. That's OK because I've used a couple of strategies that remedy this situation. The first is this: instead of making direct eye contact, focus on a visual aide. Point to your computer screen, collateral, or document, as the person you're presenting to will look at the visual aide as well. This limits eye contact and helps to diffuse any tension by taking the focus off both of you.

The second technique is indirect eye contact: instead of looking at someone squarely in the eyes, focus on the bridge of their nose or directly between the eyebrows. Oddly enough, it will appear to the person that you're making direct eye contact even though you aren't. This is a great way to look at someone without experiencing the anxiety that sometimes arises when directly meeting the eyes.

Determine if you're most comfortable siting directly across the table from someone or next to them. Sometimes, depending on the nature of the presentation, I will avoid hiding behind a desk. Instead, I'll find a more casual setting where I can sit directly next to the individual. Consider the location before starting your meeting or presentation.

One-on-one presentations are really the best way to start developing your presentation skills. As you move to larger presentations, you can lean on your one-on-one experience by focusing on just one or two individuals in your larger group until your skill and comfort level have improved. This makes for a successful transition from individual to group presentations.

Small-group presentations. I really enjoy presenting to a small group. The benefits associated with small-group presentations (when compared to a large audience) include the ease of making eye contact, improved interactions, and, of course, a much less intimidating number of people to face. Since the dynamics of a small group are different from one-on-one presentations or large-group presentations, you need to

Free resources at http://www.publicspeakingsimple.com/

consider doing a few things differently to be an effective communicator.

Make eye contact

Focus on making eye contact with each member of your audience periodically during your presentation. Some people tend to focus on a single individual but eye contact is one of the most intimate forms of connection available and should be maximized across the audience. If you find some people more engaged than others, give them more of your attention. Keep in mind that no matter who you focus on, some people will not appear engaged. Too often I see people disappointed because they didn't reach everyone in the room. Manage you expectations because no matter how engaging you may be, not everyone will give you their full attention due to issues beyond your control. It may take some time to get comfortable interacting with a small group using eye contact but your confidence will grow over time as you get more comfortable in the small group setting.

Don't read your slides word for word

If you're using a PowerPoint presentation or similar format, don't read your slides word for word. Small groups are generally less formal, and your presentation style should reflect that. Reading slides gives the impression that you aren't fully prepared and prevents the eye contact needed to engage your audience. If you find an overdependence on slides, then make notes for yourself. Don't forget that you should prepare as rigorously for a small-group presentation as you would for a large presentation. This helps to reduce your dependence on slides or a script of any kind.

Minimize distractions

Whether you're giving a one-on-one presentation or small-group presentation, do what you can to minimize distractions.

Free resources at http://www.publicspeakingsimple.com/

Ask your audience to close their laptops, shut off their iPads, and put their phones on vibrate. This request can minimize distractions and give you a better feel for how individuals are responding to your presentation through their body language and engagement. When presenting to groups that use laptops for note-taking, I usually make it a point to record the presentation (using an app like Audacity) and share it with the group along with my PowerPoint slides. Furthermore, I'll politely ask that everyone give me their full attention and assure them that I'll pause after thirty minutes for everyone to check their email. This should eliminate most of the common distractions that arise in small-group presentations. You may get some pushback or excuses but at least you made the effort.

Be mindful of the time

If you've scheduled an hour for your presentation, don't go over. It's always best to leave a little time at the end of your presentation for questions and answers (Q&A). By ending early with time for Q&A, you show others respect for their time and attendance. Furthermore, you ensure the delivery of key points on schedule while inviting participation. If you are going to need extra time, ask your audience what they prefer. Can they give you more time? Do they want to break and come back later? Are they expecting you to send the balance of your presentation via email? With small groups its best to engage them and ask how best to proceed.

Have a backup plan

What if your projector doesn't work? Do you have a backup plan? For example, I like to print copies of my presentation as a handout (two to three slides per page, double-sided) for small groups. Keep the handouts in your bag and only take them out if needed. Think through numerous aspects of your presentation and determine a fallback should things go awry. Don't assume that A/V equipment will work flawlessly or that others will provide you with what's needed. By being 100

Free resources at http://www.publicspeakingsimple.com/

percent responsible for your presentation, there's a higher probability of success.

Each of the before-mentioned techniques are essential for small-group presentations but can also be used as tools in your public speaking toolkit. Many of these techniques can also be applied to larger presentations but speaking to larger groups often involves additional techniques that account for a variety of factors.

Large-group presentations. Being successful in front of a large group of any kind surely requires a different mind-set compared to presenting one-on-one or even to small groups. Or does it? I would argue that the most effective presentation to a large group comes down to one thing and one thing only—comfort level. I know that's a pretty bold proclamation, but it embodies everything we've been talking about. If you've practiced your presentation, worked your way up through one-on-one and small-group presentations, and are a subject matter expert, why wouldn't you be comfortable? Here are a few ways to make sure your presentation to a large group is successful, building on the skills you've learned already.

Manage expectations

You're not going to have an intimate dialogue with your audience. Large-group presentations are not designed for this purpose. However, you *are* going to be making an impression on a lot of people. This is important to keep in mind as one of the main benefits of a large group presentation. When managing expectations, I like to equate a large audience to an iron. It takes a little while to heat up, but once you have got it going, it gets really hot. Focus on making an impact and building momentum throughout your presentation. Don't expect to wow everyone in the audience from the word "go." Large audiences are composed of individuals, each with their own state of mind and differing expectations. The goal is to engage

Free resources at http://www.publicspeakingsimple.com/

and communicate effectively to the majority of your audience, not every single person.

Make eye contact

Focus on making eye contact with each quadrant of the audience. Think left, right, front, and back. It's important that you don't favor a single individual or even a particular area of the room, which is sometimes tempting, depending on where you're standing on stage. If you favor one side more than another, someone is bound to feel left out. Try to make eye contact with different sections of the audience throughout the presentation. This ensures adequate coverage and improves your overall communication without placing an unrealistic expectation of trying to have a one-on-one dialog with each audience member.

Don't read your slides word for word

Regardless of the group you're presenting to, don't read your slides word for word or turn your back to the audience. This is a common practice for those not familiar with their subject matter. If you're using a PowerPoint presentation or similar type of aid, don't stand directly in front of the display or block the audience's view. Often I've seen presenters walking back and forth in front of the projector or, worse yet, turning their back to the audience completely. This is a big no-no. Pick a spot and remain there for a fixed period of time. When you reach a logical transition point, move to your next spot.

Minimize distractions

Ask your audience to turn off their mobile phones and other portable electronic devices. The master of ceremonies or person introducing you can also make this request, and it goes a long way toward eliminating interruptions. To my surprise, I've never really had an issue with distractions in a large-group setting. One would think that a larger group would generate

Free resources at http://www.publicspeakingsimple.com/

more distractions. However, I believe that large groups are generally there to hear what you have to say and are more willing to minimize distractions. Nonetheless, it is important to have someone remind the audience that mobile phones and devices should be shut off or silenced.

Be mindful of the time

If you've scheduled an hour, don't go over your allotted time. As with other presentations, it's always best to leave a little time at the end for questions and answers. By ending slightly early, you show others respect for their time and attendance and provide adequate time for meaningful dialogue with a few representative people. You will want to pace yourself using a watch or other device. Don't expect others to manage your time for you, and don't put yourself in a situation where you have to rush. When presenting to a large group, there are usually others who are presenting as well. If you go over your allotted time, it may mean less time for other speakers. Running over time is what I like to call a rookie mistake. Seasoned speakers have rehearsed their presentations down to the minute. If you run over, in my opinion, it shows that you are not prepared and not respectful of others who are speaking or the audience you're serving.

Check equipment prior to starting

It's always best to do a dry run with the tech crew prior to a large presentation. This is especially true if I need them to queue music or include audio. Never assume that a technology assistant or anyone helping you knows what to do or how to do it. Each presenter has personal preferences, so share your specific needs with anyone helping with your presentation, and be specific. Also be clear on computers, projectors, audio, visual, timings, and connections. For example, if you're using your own computer and/or monitor, bring your power cord and check for outlets. Make sure everything is in place and accounted for by doing a dry run prior to the live event.

Free resources at http://www.publicspeakingsimple.com/

Use a clicker to advance your slides

Having to walk back and forth to the podium to advance your slides can detract from the overall presentation flow. Find a clicker that you like and one that provides adequate range. It can smooth out your presentation and create flawless timing. I found a great quality wireless clicker on Amazon.com that I've been using for years to advance my slides and improve my presentations. It has become an integral part of all my presentations and I never leave home without it. Regardless of what type of clicker you select, set it up prior to the presentation, not the day of. Software installation may be necessary for the device to be operational.

Decide what kind of speaker you are

This sounds more like a strategy than a technique but is important when preparing for a large group presentation. Will you stand behind the podium? Will you meander across the stage? Will you use a lapel microphone or a handheld microphone? Will you use a PowerPoint or simply speak without visuals? These are all important factors to consider before you ever step onto the stage and are part of why it is so important to work your way up to this kind of presentation. In most situations, prior experience helps define the type of presenter you are and the preferences that work best for you. If you personally don't have the benefit of prior experience before being asked to present to a large audience, consider the options that may ease your anxiety.

Expect to be nervous at first

I still get a bit of stage fright before stepping in front of hundreds of people, but I've relabeled that feeling as excitement. So get excited and give it your best! Even if you've mastered the art of public speaking, addressing a large audience can be a bit overwhelming at first. The dynamic is different from any other presentation type, so you may

Free resources at http://www.publicspeakingsimple.com/

experience some of the same feelings you experienced earlier in your development. Anticipating this diffuses any uncomfortable feelings you may have. The thrilling part of large groups is that by addressing the needs of a large audience, you can deliver a presentation that makes a lasting impact. Large presentations require the culmination and application of skills you've worked hard to develop but are very rewarding.

Don't ignore the special needs of a large group compared to one-on-one or small group presentations and always check the criteria above before moving forward. Large presentations are unique and require the culmination and application of skills you've worked hard to develop. In addition to one-on-one, small group, and large group presentations, you may experience other presentation formats.

Online and Web-Based Formats

In addition to giving live presentations, technology affords us the ability to present from distant locations. In particular the use of Skype and webinar platforms (such as GoToMeeting and Webex) allow us to present to audiences in real time anywhere, from anywhere. Although I'm somewhat embarrassed to admit it, I've actually given presentations from highway rest stops, hotel rooms, and coffee bars. It's best to give your presentation from a quiet location but as long as you have an Internet connection and access to a web-based presentation tool, you can make it work.

When presenting via Skype, Google Hangout, GoToMeeting, Webex, or another broadcasting tool, there are a number of factors to consider. Skype and Google Hangout are video-conferencing tools that allow you to speak directly to others using video chat, audio only, or screen share. When using these tools, it's important to check your Internet connection before starting and make sure, if using video, you look your best. Don't forget to make appropriate eye contact if using the

Free resources at http://www.publicspeakingsimple.com/

video option. Making eye contact in this situation may mean looking directly into your computer's camera or webcam, not at the face of the individual on screen. This became apparent to me after watching the replay of my Skype interview with Sharyn Alfonsi from *ABC World News*. Even though I was looking at her on my screen, from the audience's perspective I was looking down at my feet. Not my best moment in public speaking but a valuable lesson that has improved my video-conferencing skills tremendously.

As always, minimize distractions when using video conferencing and test your sound levels before the actual interview or presentation. All of these tools require adequate bandwidth to run properly. It's best to attempt a dry run with a friend or colleague before using tools like Skype, Google Hangout, or any other type of video related technology. Preparation is essential, not only of your material but the technology used to deliver your presentation as well.

GoToMeeting and Webex are very popular for giving presentations online. Depending on which features you have enabled, you may choose to let others see you via webcam or to share your computer screen. This is still considered public speaking because you're presenting to one or more people and it requires that you apply many of the same techniques we've been discussing for a powerful presentation.

The reason people use GoToMeeting, Webex, JoinMe, and a whole host of online meeting tools is to share a slide presentation or website navigation. Doing a demo of a website adds a layer of complexity to your presentation because, in addition to knowing what you're going to say, you must also be confident in your ability to navigate a website in a prescribed order. The only way to ensure a quality presentation is through rehearsal, don't wing it! I encourage you to go back to the rule of four. Rehearse four hours for every one hour you plan to present either online or offline. Combine navigation with your script or outline to get comfortable with this unique presentation

Free resources at http://www.publicspeakingsimple.com/

style. The more Webex presentations you give the more proficient you will become.

When preparing for webinars and other online presentations, I like to spend the early part of my rehearsal getting the navigation down pat. If you repeat navigation over and over again, it becomes second nature, allowing you to focus on what you're saying in the presentation. Preparing navigation and what you're saying at the same time may be difficult to master. I found that focusing on navigation and later rehearsing the speech makes for a much smoother process. Find what works best for you, practicing both navigation and the verbal content.

Public Speaking Made Simple strategies

Throughout this book I've shared with you a number of techniques that took me many years to develop in order to overcome my fear of public speaking and become more confident when delivering a presentation, large or small. I think it's vitally important to mention that, although I personally use these techniques on a regular basis, they may not work "as is" for every individual. Rather, consider them strategies designed to get you going in the right direction on the path to public speaking success. Make them fit your individual style and personality.

In this section I'd like to reiterate many of the techniques I've shared with you and cover some of the nuance associated with each of them. Consider this as both summary and launching pad for those serious about gaining confidence or improving their speaking ability.

Rehearse in your mind. Did you know that most successful people envisioned their success long before it materialized in their physical world? The same is true when it comes to areas that we want to improve in our own lives. If you visualize your success again and again, you can overcome many of the

Free resources at http://www.publicspeakingsimple.com/

obstacles traditionally associated with public speaking. I know that sounds like hocus pocus if you're not into visualization, but it works because you're changing your paradigm.

I started using this technique shortly after attending my first Toastmasters meeting. Each night before drifting off to sleep, I would see myself standing confidently in front of the audience and giving a strong, effective presentation with a big smile on my face. Although I had read a great deal about visualization, it was never something that I applied in my own life until trying to improve my public speaking. By rehearsing my optimal performance in my mind over and over again, it changed my perception of what was possible and how I viewed myself. If it hadn't been for the constant repetition, I don't know if I would have ever seen myself differently. What I find most amazing is that now it's hard for me to imagine things negatively. Trying to see myself as a nervous wreck or an unprofessional speaker just doesn't compute anymore.

What most people won't tell you about visualization is that some people have an easier time with it than others. It took me a few weeks before I was able to see myself as being truly confident. Over time visualization of what I really wanted got easier, and the effects were impressive. Each time I found myself standing in front of a group or audience, I became noticeably more at ease and comfortable inside my own body, exuding a confidence I had never experienced before.

The key with any technique, especially visualization, is to stay the course. In today's society everyone wants immediate results, and who can blame them? But demanding immediate results usually ends in failure. Results obtained in an instant can be lost in the same amount of time. For lasting change you must start slowly down a path and follow it until it becomes habit, second nature. Visualization works the same way. It may be difficult and even challenging in the beginning, but it gets significantly easier over time. The best part of using visualization is that it pays huge dividends and doesn't require

Free resources at http://www.publicspeakingsimple.com/

the same level of effort once you've achieved a breakthrough. It's important that you start now, even if you do so by watching other speakers at first.

As you begin watching other speakers, imagine yourself in their place. In your mind's eye, become the person you want to be. As you burn this image into your subconscious, you'll find that your comfort level and overall behavior is vastly improved when you're in real speaking situations. Don't underestimate the power of visualization. To be effective, set aside time daily to apply the technique and imagine yourself as a confident, engaging, and effective presenter. Take advantage of downtime—either before going to bed, over your morning cup of coffee, or sitting in a waiting room. Consciously integrate the technique into your daily routine and you'll have a head start on addressing and eliminating your fear.

Begin with a goal. One of the reasons people are so fearful of public speaking is because they are usually focused on their own anxiety, standing in front of a group of strangers, instead of on a particular goal. When giving a presentation, your focus should be on your audience, not yourself. This is a mistake I see repeated over and over again. When students critique themselves, I rarely hear, "The audience wasn't engaged." Rather I hear something like, "I felt so anxious." Or "I forgot to say X, Y, and Z." Begin by asking yourself what the primary purpose of your presentation actually is. Are you trying to educate people about a particular topic? Are you attempting to illustrate a specific point? What is the takeaway for the audience? When you focus on the viewers and clarify expectations, much of the pressure you feel is refocused to where it should be, on those who came to listen to you.

One of the techniques I continue to use with each presentation is starting with a goal. My goal may be simply to entertain an audience or, more common, communicate or explain something effectively. Having a goal keeps me on track and lessens my anxiety. You know your material and your audience better than anyone. Think about your goal and what you want to achieve.

Make sure your goal is both reasonable and attainable. Some people set lofty goals without a clear roadmap for getting there. I'm not saying you should aim low. Rather, find goals that are a stretch for you but you believe are attainable.

Preparation. If you take away only one thing from this book, make sure it's adequate preparation. I'm sharing this with you based on years of experience, trial and error, and overcoming my own fear of public speaking. I've been making presentations for a long time and still prepare by using the rule of four to ensure my success. Keep in mind that when you watch others make a flawless presentation, you are not seeing the hours of preparation and rehearsal completed behind the scenes. Whether their preparation was directly related to the presentation you saw or a culmination of hours of previous presentations, those speakers didn't wake up one morning, step onto the stage, and become someone like Tony Robbins. It takes significant practice, hard work, repetition, and focus.

I used to think that I was different and didn't need to prepare—especially when the content was familiar to me or where a good deal of time was already dedicated to working on PowerPoint slides. But there really aren't any exceptions to the rule. Everyone must prepare if they want to be successful. It's true that if you're delivering the same exact presentation over and over again, the rule of four may fall by the wayside. However, I would argue that, to keep your audiences engaged and yourself interested, you should always be thinking of ways to improve and customize your presentation. This is what makes good even better.

Expect to transition. The process of moving from fearful to confident is simple but not always easy. As you begin your journey, don't forget that everyone gets a little anxious about change. But remember: this is change for the better. It's

Free resources at http://www.publicspeakingsimple.com/

guaranteed to make you a more confident, effective person in many aspects of your life beyond public speaking. When we talked about relabeling your anxiety as excitement, we also discussed that it takes a while before the change becomes permanent. It may be some time before you are genuinely excited about presenting. Your only job initially is to stay the course. If you expect some anxiety and accept the fact that change happens gradually, you'll have a much easier time making the adjustment to the new you.

Some people will have an easier time with their transition than others, due in large part to the amount of effort they put into the process (preparation and mindset) while others need to go at a slower pace. This is why it's difficult to answer the question, "How long does it take?" It all depends on you. I've seen people determined to overcome their fear jump in with both feet. Six weeks later, after changing their mind-set, attending Toastmasters, and practicing, they're practically different people. Others take longer either because they have a longer timeline for their goals or simply because they have more adjustments to make. To alleviate your anxiety about change, I recommend sitting down and writing a plan for your transition. Begin by grading yourself as a public speaker on a scale of one to ten. Where are you now? Where do you want to be? By when? And most importantly, what's your plan for getting there? What techniques are you going to use and how often? Last, stick to your plan and record your successes along the way. You can do this!

Breathe. We've talked about the power of breath. Proper breathing is one of the most effective ways to be physically calm in uncertain situations. In addition to preparation, proper breathing is essential for public speaking success. In addition to practicing proper breathing techniques, don't be afraid to slow down the pace of your presentation. A common mistake for new speakers is racing through their material, especially when being interviewed. As I began to videotape different types of presentations I had made, I discovered just how quickly I was speaking. In fact, it became apparent that my perception

Free resources at http://www.publicspeakingsimple.com/

of pacing was different from how it appeared to the audience. Take time to answer questions or make a statement, whatever you do, don't rush. You may think that your responses seem lethargic, but more often than not, they don't come across that way. If you watch professionals being interviewed, they generally take the time to fully listen to a question, pause, and then begin speaking instead of blurting out an answer. Practice proper breathing and slow the overall pace of your presentation. This gives you more time to think and eases tension.

Have a presentation checklist. Take ten minutes the day before you present and review your to-do list. The list below is by no means comprehensive but should get you started on things to consider. You want to make sure all of the big items are out of the way so you can focus on delivering a great presentation:

- Hard copies of your presentation
- Presentation on flash drive (cloud backup)
- Introduction for MC
- Clicker
- Laptop
- Projector
- Microphone
- Bottled water
- Internet access if needed

Free resources at http://www.publicspeakingsimple.com/

Add to this list and keep it in a safe place. You should review this checklist to ensure that all of the necessary equipment and content is available for your presentation. Knowing that you have the major items addressed will help to lessen your anxiety.

Get started. The only way to change is to take action. Reading alone doesn't make it happen. With other how-to books I've published, I occasionally hear from readers something along the lines of "I've read your book ten times, but change hasn't happened yet." To start seeing improvements, you must take the first step. Begin with a single technique and start to apply it. Ask yourself why this change is a must for you and find the motivation you need to take one small step. Through repetition and effort, change will happen. Find a mentor to help you and hold you accountable. If you are not comfortable with a mentor it may be easier to find a presentation buddy—someone else who is struggling with public speaking and is on the path to confidence.

At the very least, I strongly recommend that you find someone whom you can rehearse with. When you make the transition from self-rehearsal to practicing in front of an individual, it's advisable to work with someone you know instead of a complete stranger. The familiarity and trust help get you started. Apply whatever resources you need—just get started today.

Remember to focus on progress, not perfection. Your fear of public speaking wasn't created in a day and the same can be true for the remedy. Slow and steady wins the race. Also, when you focus on making improvements over time, the pressure you feel to get things exactly as they "should" be is greatly diminished. As mentioned earlier, I think it's important to have a goal each time you speak. Perhaps your goal can be focused on improving the pace of your presentation, using your notes less, or simply improving your breathing. Always try to

Free resources at http://www.publicspeakingsimple.com/

do something better than you did during your previous presentation. Look to make small improvements over time to enhance your skills and build your confidence. It all begins with taking that first step which you've already done by reading this book. The next step is up to you.

Conclusion

I have to admit, I'm truly excited for you. Improving your confidence, becoming an effective speaker, and changing your life for the better lies in your future. I feel blessed to share with you what I've learned from my public speaking journey. Although each person starts from a unique place, my goal is the same for everyone, to feel more confident and secure when presenting to others. I hope that the path for you is now clearly within reach. If you ever stumble on your journey, remember that many others have taken this path and succeeded, and you will too. As I've said throughout, often the only difference between success and failure is that people who fail give up too soon. Remember that whatever you're ailment: fear, anxiety, inexperience, there is a remedy. Apply the *Public Speaking Made Simple* techniques we've discussed throughout this guide to improve your skills and confidence. I know that if you use your mind, prepare, rehearse, use positive self-talk, and apply proper breathing techniques, confidence will be yours for the taking.

A Simple Request

I like feedback. My goal is to provide life-changing information that can help you realize your full potential. Please share your thoughts by leaving a book review on **Amazon.com**. To each person who leaves a review, I'm happy to send a copy of *The Top Five Public Speaking Pitfalls and How to Avoid Them* absolutely FREE ($47 value). Just send a link to your review to support@publicspeakingsimple.com.

Visit publicspeakingsimple.com for additional tools, resources, and information

Free resources at http://www.publicspeakingsimple.com/

www.ingramcontent.com/pod-product-compliance
Lightning Source LLC
Chambersburg PA
CBHW071725040426
42446CB00011B/2216